FROM EDEN TO BABEL

INTERNATIONAL THEOLOGICAL COMMENTARY

Fredrick Carlson Holmgren and George A. F. Knight

General Editors

FROM EDEN TO BABEL

A *Commentary on the Book of*

Genesis 1-11

DONALD E. GOWAN

WM. B. EERDMANS PUBLISHING CO., GRAND RAPIDS

THE HANDSEL PRESS LTD, EDINBURGH

Copyright © 1988 by William B. Eerdmans Publishing Company
First published 1988 by William B. Eerdmans Publishing Company,
255 Jefferson Ave. S.E., Grand Rapids, Michigan 49503
and
The Handsel Press Limited
33 Montgomery Street, Edinburgh EH7 5JX

Library of Congress Cataloging-in-Publication Data

Gowan, Donald E.
From Eden to Babel: a commentary on the book of Genesis 1–11 /
Donald E. Gowan
p.   cm.   —(International theological commentary)
Bibliography: p. 124
ISBN 0-8028-0337-7
1. Bible. O.T. Genesis I–XI—Criticism, interpretation, etc.
I. Title. II. Series.
BS1235.2.G68   1988
222′.1107—dc19   88-11271
CIP

Eerdmans ISBN 0-8028-0337-7
Handsel ISBN 0 905312 85 6

CONTENTS

ABBREVIATIONS

KJV	King James (Authorized) Version
NEB	New English Bible
RSV	Revised Standard Version
TEV	Today's English Version

EDITORS' PREFACE

The Old Testament alive in the Church: this is the goal of the *International Theological Commentary.* Arising out of changing, unsettled times, this Scripture speaks with an authentic voice to our own troubled world. It witnesses to God's ongoing purpose and to his caring presence in the universe without ignoring those experiences of life that cause one to question his existence and love. This commentary series is written by front-rank scholars who treasure the life of faith.

Addressed to ministers and Christian educators, the *International Theological Commentary* moves beyond the usual critical-historical approach to the Bible and offers a *theological* interpretation of the Hebrew text. Thus, engaging larger textual units of the biblical writings, the authors of these volumes assist the reader in the appreciation of the theology underlying the text as well as its place in the thought of the Hebrew Scriptures. But more, since the Bible is the book of the believing community, its text has acquired ever more meaning through an ongoing interpretation. This growth of interpretation may be found both within the Bible itself and in the continuing scholarship of the Church.

Contributors to the *International Theological Commentary* are Christians—persons who affirm the witness of the New Testament concerning Jesus Christ. For Christians, the Bible is *one* Scripture containing the Old and New Testaments. For this reason, a commentary on the Old Testament may not ignore the second part of the canon, namely, the New Testament.

Since its beginning, the Church has recognized a special relationship between the two Testaments. But the precise character of this bond has been difficult to define. The diversity of views represented in these publications makes us aware that the Church is not of one mind in expressing the "how" of this relationship. The authors of this series share a developing consensus that any serious explanation of the Old Testament's relationship to the New will uphold the integrity of the Old Testament. Even though Christianity is rooted in the soil of the Hebrew Scriptures, the biblical interpreter must take care lest he "christianize" these Scriptures.

Authors writing in this commentary series will, no doubt, hold various views concerning *how* the Old Testament relates to the New. No attempt has been made to dictate one viewpoint in this matter. With the whole Church, we are convinced that the relationship between the two Testaments is real and substantial. But we recognize also the diversity of opinions among Christian scholars when they attempt to articulate fully the nature of this relationship.

In addition to the Christian Church, there exists another people for whom the Old Testament is important, namely, the Jewish community. Both Jews and Christians claim the Hebrew Bible as Scripture. Jews believe that the basic teachings of this Scripture point toward, and are developed by, the Talmud, which assumed its present form about 500 C.E. On the other hand, Christians hold that the Old Testament finds its fulfillment in the New Testament. The Hebrew Bible, therefore, belongs to both the Church and the Synagogue.

Recent studies have demonstrated how profoundly early Christianity reflects a Jewish character. This fact is not surprising because the Christian movement arose out of the context of first-century Judaism. Further, Jesus himself was Jewish, as were the first Christians. It is to be expected, therefore, that Jewish and Christian interpretations of the Hebrew Bible will reveal similarities *and* disparities. Such is the case. The authors of the *International Theological Commentary* will refer to the various Jewish traditions that they consider important for an appreciation of the Old Testament text. Such references will enrich our understanding of certain biblical passages and, as an extra gift, offer us insight into the relationship of Judaism to early Christianity.

An important second aspect of the present series is its *international* character. In the past, Western church leaders were considered to be *the* leaders of the Church—at least by those living in the West! The theology and biblical exegesis done by these scholars dominated the thinking of the Church. Most commentaries were produced in the Western world and reflected the lifestyle, needs, and thoughts of its civilization. But the Christian Church is a worldwide community. People who belong to the universal Church reflect differing thoughts, needs, and lifestyles.

Today the fastest-growing churches in the world are to be found, not in the West, but in Africa, Indonesia, South America, Korea, Taiwan, and elsewhere. By the end of the century, Christians in these areas will outnumber those who live in the West. In our age, especially, a commentary on the Bible must transcend the parochialism of Western civilization and be sensitive to issues that are the special problems of persons who live outside the "Christian" West, issues such as race relations, personal survival and fulfillment, liberation, revolution, famine, tyranny, disease, war, the poor, religion, and state. Inspired by God, the authors of the Old Testament knew what life is like on the edge of existence. They addressed themselves to everyday people who often faced more than everyday problems. Refusing to limit God to the "spiritual," they portrayed him as one who heard and knew the cries of people in pain (see Exod. 3:7-8). The contributors to the *International Theological Commentary* are persons who prize the writings of these biblical authors as a word of life to our world today. They read the Hebrew Scriptures in the contexts of ancient Israel and our modern day.

The scholars selected as contributors underscore the international aspect of the Commentary. Representing very different geographical, ideological, and ecclesiastical backgrounds, they come from over seventeen countries. Besides scholars from such traditional countries as England, Scotland, France, Italy, Switzerland, Canada, New Zealand, Australia, South Africa, and the United States, contributors from the following places are included: Israel, Indonesia, India, Thailand, Singapore, Taiwan, and countries of Eastern Europe. Such diversity makes for richness of thought. Christian scholars living in Buddhist, Muslim, or Socialist lands may be able to offer the World Church insights into the biblical message—insights to which the scholarship of the West could be blind.

The proclamation of the biblical message is the focal concern of the *International Theological Commentary*. Generally speaking, the authors of these commentaries value the historical-critical studies of past scholars, but they are convinced that these studies by themselves are not enough. The Bible is more than an object of critical study; it is the revelation of God. In the written Word, God has disclosed himself and his will to humankind. Our authors see themselves as servants of the Word which, when rightly received, brings *shalom* to both the individual and the community.

—George A. F. Knight
—Fredrick Carlson Holmgren

INTRODUCTION

Genesis 1–11 in the Pentateuch

The first eleven chapters of Genesis are like nothing else in the Bible. For the most part, Scripture focuses on places, events, people, and dates that are a part of the known history of humanity. The OT speaks primarily of and to Israel, and the NT's revelation in Jesus Christ is addressed first to the Jews, the descendants of that same Israel. But Israel is not mentioned in Gen. 1–11 and indeed does not exist even in anticipation in those stories, for the anticipation clearly begins only in 12:1-3. Although the places we can identify (Ararat, Babel, Canaan, etc.) are all to be found in the Middle East, none of the individuals named and none of the events described can be found in the records of the ancient civilizations of that region. Things happen in these chapters that are far removed not only from our own experiences but also from the kinds of events described in the rest of the Bible. There exists on earth a forbidden tree, a snake talks, Cain bears a mark that protects him from harm, a flood covers the entire earth including its highest mountains, and people live to be nine hundred years old. No wonder people ask, Are these myths? Are these fairy stories? Are these tales for children? The answer is yes, they are tales for children . . . and adults—especially adults. They are not myths, not fairy tales. But neither are they "Bible history." For they are clearly different from the history that the Bible records elsewhere, as the OT itself will show us.

The Pentateuch has a theme that holds its varied parts together, the promise of the land of Canaan to the descendants of Abraham. It is first given in Gen. 12:7, and it is frequently repeated (cf. Exod. 6:3-8; Lev. 26:40-45; Num. 32:11; Deut. 1:6-8; 29:2-9). Near the end of the Pentateuch a summary of God's mighty acts in history on behalf of Israel is given in a form that has been called a "historical credo" (Deut. 26:5-9). It begins with a brief allusion to the stories of the patriarchs in Gen. 12–50 ("A wandering Aramean was my father; and he went down into Egypt and sojourned there . . .") and concludes with the occupation of Canaan, which is to be the next act in Israel's history from the perspective of Deuteronomy. This summarizes the historical parts of the Pentateuch, with the exception of Gen. 1–11 and the experience at Sinai (which need not concern us). Those first chapters are different. As far as Gen. 12–50, Exodus, Leviticus, Numbers, and Deuteronomy are concerned, they need not be present. These books contain no references to Adam and Eve, Cain and Abel, Enoch, or Noah, or the Flood. Of the themes in Gen. 1–11 only creation is alluded to (cf. Deut. 4:32; 32:6). Gen. 1–11 stands as a separate unit, a preface to the history of salvation, which begins with Gen. 12, and a preface to which the authors of the OT felt little need to refer, for some reason.

Despite the discontinuity of themes and characters between Gen. 1–11 and the rest of the Pentateuch, modern scholarship has found one type of continuity running through these books. If we ask whether the first eleven chapters were composed by a different author and later added to the Pentateuch as a preface, scholarship's answer is negative. There is evidence for a continuity of authorship. Gen. 1–11 seems to have been composed of two sources that continue through the rest of Genesis into Exodus, Leviticus, and Numbers. For example, the same style, vocabulary, and interests reappear in Gen. 1, 17; Exod. 6; and the whole book of Leviticus, to mention only a few of its occurrences. This is the source called P, because of its strong "priestly" interests. A distinctively different style appears in Gen. 2–4, 15; Exod. 32; and Num. 12, to select a few examples. It has been denoted J (from the German spelling, "Jahweh"), since in Genesis it is the only source that uses the divine name of God, "Yahweh." If these source critical analyses are correct, and most scholars still accept them in spite of many challenges, then it means that two different authors in Israel, living in different periods (for J is dated in the 10th cent. B.C. and P in the 6th or 5th), both thought it necessary to begin their works with this special kind of material. Where they got that material and what it was like when they found it will be discussed briefly in the Commentary. It will be seen that what became of it after it was written in Scripture is more important theologically than where it came from. The testimony of both P and J is that although this material is different, it belongs. They do not tell us why they believed it belonged; we must consider the relationship of Gen. 1–11 to the rest of the Bible in order to determine that.

It may be helpful first to survey briefly what happens in these chapters. Here is a sketchy outline.

Ch. 1   God creates the world and everything in it.

Ch. 2   God plants a garden where the first couple live; in it is a tree from which they are forbidden to eat.

Ch. 3   They eat from the tree; as a result, life becomes much harder for them and they are expelled from the garden.

Ch. 4   Sibling rivalry, murder, wandering, city-building, technology.

Ch. 5   A genealogy; nothing happens.

6:1-4   Cohabitation of sons of gods with daughters of men.

6:5–8:22   Universal wickedness leads to a universal Flood; only one family is saved.

9:1-17   God promises never again to send a flood to destroy the whole earth.

9:18-29   Drunkenness, disrespect for parents, cursing.

Ch. 10   A listing of the population of the whole earth.

Ch. 11   More city-building, confusion of language, dispersion into all parts of the earth; a genealogy leads to the time of Abraham.

In brief, these chapters depict movement from a world none of us has ever known toward the real world of human history. In the world we have *not* known, everything is all right, in accord with the will of God. In the real world, some things are all right, but dissension, oppression, violence, and pain also abound. It is not difficult to see why both P and J found it necessary to use this kind of material as the preface to their histories of salvation. It describes a world in which salvation is necessary.

Genesis 1–11 in the Bible

Israel seems to have kept most of the subject matter of Gen. 1–11 compartmentalized. These chapters existed as part of their sacred writings, but the authors of the OT do not draw upon them, except for the teaching that Yahweh, God of Israel, was Creator of the heavens and the earth. Other prominent creation texts, in addition to Gen. 1–2, are Job 38–41; Pss. 8, 33, 74, 104, 136, 148; Prov. 8:22-31; and many passages in Isa. 40–66. Ezra's prayer in Neh. 9:6-31 adds creation to the traditional recital of the mighty acts of God. As an eschatological hope developed, it included the promise of a new creation, from which all the corruptions of sin and evil would be removed (Isa. 65:17-25; 66:22-23).

The OT contains many other brief references to the creator God, but outside of the genealogy in 1 Chr. 1, the only explicit references to Gen. 1–11 are Isa. 54:9, which speaks of Noah and the Flood; Ps. 78:51; 105:23, 27; 106:22, which refer to Ham; and Josh. 24:2, which mentions Terah. The other themes of the preface to salvation history, which were developed so extensively and with such great effect in later history, were allowed to lie virtually dormant during the OT period. Perhaps this was because most of the OT message focuses on the relationship between God and Israel, while Gen. 1–11 deals with God and humanity as a whole. That was important enough for these chapters to keep their place as a preface, but not enough for them to be developed and woven into the story of God's dealings with his people Israel.

In contrast to the OT, the Jewish literature produced during the period between ca. 200 B.C. and ca. A.D. 100 shows a great interest in interpreting and applying the teachings of Gen. 1–11. This was Holy Scripture for the Jews, and it spoke of matters of great importance to them. They still considered themselves to be the chosen people, living in a special covenant relationship with God; but the nation Israel, with its own territory, culture, and government, had not existed for a long time, and the Jews had learned to live their faith in the midst of other cultures. As a result, their outlook had broadened and what Scripture said about humanity as a whole had become more important to them.

One way for the Jews of this period to apply Scripture to their own time was to retell it, resolving difficulties as they did so and including essential doctrines where they had not appeared before. A good example of this is the book of Jubilees, which devotes chs. 2–12 to retelling Gen. 1–11. Similar efforts appear in the Genesis Apocryphon found at Qumran and in Pseudo-Philo. Briefer retellings appear in the surveys of history found in apocalyptic literature (e.g., 1 En. 85-89; 2 Bar. 56), in Sirach's praise of famous men (Sir. 44:16-18), and in other types of literature.

Creation theology continued to appear in a prominent way as Jews affirmed their monotheistic faith over against the beliefs in many gods characteristic of the dominant cultures in which they lived (e.g., Wisd. 16; Song of the Three Young Men; Jub. 2; 1 En. 2:1–5:3; 17–36, 41; 2 En. 24–25; 47:3-6). The chief events of interest are the fall of Adam and Eve (2 En. 31; Jub. 3:17-35; 2 Esdr. 7:10-11, 46-56 [116-126]; 2 Bar. 23:4; 56:5-6; Apoc. Abraham 23), the cohabitation of the sons of the gods with the daughters of men alluded to in Gen. 6:1-4 (Wisd. 14:6; Sir. 16:7; 1 En. 6–10,

15, 86–88; Sib. Or. 1:65-124; 2 Bar. 56:10-15; 3 Macc. 2:4; Damascus Document 2:18-21; 3:1), and the Flood (Wisd. 10:4; Sir. 40:10; 44:17-18; 1 En. 89; Sib. Or. 1:125-280; 3 Macc. 2:4; 4 Macc. 15:31-32). Enoch, whose treatment in the OT amounts to only four verses (Gen. 5:21-24), took on great importance in the intertestamental period. Since he "walked with God; and he was not, for God took him," it was thought he had special access to the secrets of heaven and earth, past and future, and was not only exalted as a righteous man (Sir. 44:16; 49:14) but was also made the pseudonymous author of apocalyptic books (1 and 2 Enoch). In short, by 200 B.C. the stories in Gen. 1–11 had captured the imaginations of Jews, as they have done for virtually every reader since, and the writers of this period found in them material of great theological value.

This survey of intertestamental literature helps explain why the NT makes more use of Gen. 1–11 than does the entire OT. It had become customary for Jewish authors to do so by the 1st cent. A.D., and the writers of the NT found much of theological value in those chapters. Creation theology is reaffirmed and given an entirely new dimension by means of Christology. God has revealed himself through creation (Rom. 1:20), which is not evil in itself, for God made it to be good (1 Tim. 4:1-5). He created all things through his eternal Son (Col. 1:15-20; Heb. 1:2), the Word (John 1:1-18), whose death and resurrection have made possible the inbreaking of the new creation, which can already be experienced by those who believe in him (2 Cor. 5:17; Gal. 6:15; Eph. 4:22-24; Col. 3:9-10), although the consummation of God's intention for his world is still awaited (Rev. 21–22).

The fall of Adam and Eve became a key element in Paul's theology, distinguishing his thinking from other Jewish writers of the time. From Gen. 3 he developed the concept of original sin: "Therefore as sin came into the world through one man and death through sin, and so death spread to all men because all men sinned . . ." (Rom. 5:12). In contrast to the first Adam, from whom came death, he places Christ as the Second Adam, from whom comes life (Rom. 5:12-21).

Eve is mentioned in an unfortunate way, in support of male supremacy, in 1 Tim. 2:12-14. Cain and Abel have become clear-cut examples of wicked and righteous behavior (Matt. 23:35; Heb. 11:4; 1 John 3:12; Jude 11), and both Enoch and Noah have also become moral examples (Heb. 11:5-7; 2 Pet. 2:5). The Flood became both a type of baptism (1 Pet. 3:20) and of the second coming (Matt. 24:37-39). But surely the most profound effect that the NT use of Gen. 1–11 had on Christian theology was Paul's interpretation of the fall as having brought sin and death into the world for all people.

Genesis 1–11 in Synagogue and Church

These chapters have continued to play an important role in the thinking of Jews and Christians to this day, and have always been one of the best known parts of the Bible. From the early part of the Common Era, Genesis Rabbah provides a good example of the midrashic interpretation widely used in Jewish teaching. Both Jews and Christians continued to develop the doctrine of creation, using Gen. 1 as their basic text. Christians, however, made more use of Gen. 1–3 as a resource for their doctrine of humanity. Throughout Christian history extensive discussion has focused on the "image of God" in which humans were created (Gen. 1:26-27)—of what the image consists and whether it was lost in the fall. This took on a greater importance for Christians than for Jews because of Paul's references to Christ as the image of God (Col. 1:15) and because of his teaching that in Christ humans may be conformed to his image (Rom. 8:29; 1 Cor. 15:49; Col. 3:10), which suggests something not indicated in the OT; that in the fall the image of God in humans was lost or distorted.

The doctrine of the fall and the associated teachings concerning original sin and total depravity, which have been extensively debated throughout the history of the Church, have been based largely on Gen. 1 and 3, read through the eyes of NT writers and supported by certain other OT texts (e.g., Ps. 51:5). These beliefs have had a profound effect on the theology and worship of the Church (e.g., on the understanding of baptism), and they have made the Christian outlook on human potential rather different from that of the Jews. Judaism did not develop so distinct a concept of "fall" and remained more optimistic in general about the ability to obey God. The Jews found the source of sin in the "evil inclination," part of God's good creation that could be misused, leading to sin; but they believed that diligent study of the Torah provided an effective means to overcome it.

Early Christian interpreters looked everywhere in the OT for messianic prophecies, and some thought they found the earliest one in Gen. 3:15. The "seed" of the woman, who will bruise the serpent's heel, was said to be Christ, who will defeat Satan. This became a part of Christian tradition, even though there have always been some scholars who did not accept it. The allegorical method of interpretation, which remained standard in the Church from the early days until the Reformation, was able to find Christian doctrine in virtually any OT text. The rejection of allegory by the Reformers of the 16th cent. did not lead to any diminution of the importance of these chapters, however, for both Martin Luther and John Calvin wrote long commentaries on them, staying very close to the literal meaning of the text.

As these chapters had become one of the most important parts of the OT for Christian theology, so they became the major battleground, in the 19th cent., of the conflict between traditional interpretations of Scripture and the newly appearing scientific and historical worldviews. The Church was confronted with questions that new information about the world made it necessary to take seriously for the first time: Was the earth created in 4004 B.C., or is it billions of years old? How can creation in six days be reconciled with geological explanations of the earth's strata? Can a universal flood be explained by scientific means? How can we account for the fantastically long lives attributed to the people in Gen. 5? Frequently the battle between science and religion, which has not yet been completely quelled, focused on Gen. 1–11, and for many Christians those chapters became either an embarrassment to be explained away somehow or a rallying point to be defended to the last, rather than the source of nourishment to the faith that they once had been. One of the aims of this commentary is to try to avoid attack, apology, and defense in order to show how scholarship late in this 20th cent. can help us find nourishment once again.

Until the methods of modern science were developed, it was simply assumed that all the information in Gen. 1–11, of whatever kind, was accurate. The discoveries of science about the age and formation of the world made it necessary to ask whether there are not different kinds of information, various realms of truth. The question still debated is whether a document that contains historical or scientific inaccuracies can be the inspired Word of God, completely reliable as theological truth. My position is that it can. Form criticism is one of the modern scholarly approaches to the Bible that helps us to see how that is possible.

Form criticism studies the uses of distinct types of speech to convey specific kinds of information, appropriate for particular situations. It has taught us, for example, that we should not expect a parable to use only real historical characters and situations in order to be "true." It is not so hard to agree that one is permitted to make up a completely fictional story, such as a parable, in order to convey truth. Form criticism has identified the subjects of most of the stories in Genesis not as fiction, but as *typical* events, which tend to recur generation after generation rather than being unique to one time and place. It concludes that this kind of literature was told not just to re- call the past but to help one understand one's own encounter with the same realities. These stories could function as self-affirmations in many different times and places. So, the story of Eve and Adam in the garden speaks not just of one temptation and sin, but is recog- nizable as an accurate description of the same process we have expe- rienced when we ourselves have given in to temptation. The story of Cain and Abel includes among its elements the issue of sibling rivalry, with which anyone who has brothers and sisters can identify. In our terms, some of the recurring issues that make these *our* sto- ries, and not just tales of the distant past, are: humans and the natu- ral environment, tensions between the sexes, breakdowns of family relations, violent solutions to human problems, the threat of world destruction, and the threat of too much concentration of human power.

Stories of this type have been called *sagas* in most of the form criti- cal literature, but that is probably a misuse of the Scandinavian word. There is no obviously preferable term, so in this book I have called them *archetypal stories*, as a reminder of their function. Other types of literature are found in these chapters, mainly lists and the account of creation (which is not an event that is repeated), but the stories all function to some extent in the manner described above. As Amos N. Wilder has commented:

> We can say that the ancient patterns of rehearsal in the Bible— these genealogies of heaven and earth, these paradigms of the human family, these vicissitudes of a pilgrim people through ancient economies, these records of conscience in the making, these annals of man's generic passions, his wrestlings with the angel, the pride and miscarriage of his works and many inven- tions—we can say that these ancient rehearsals may be recog- nized in some sort as the archetypal molds of our own histo- ries and fabulations. In these tracks our own courses are run.

> (*Jesus' Parables and the War of Myths:*
> *Essays on Imagination in the Scripture*
> [Philadelphia: Fortress and London: SPCK, 1982], 51)

At this point it is appropriate to say something about inspiration. This introduction has focused on activities of human authors, inter- preters, and believing communities. In these archetypal stories the human factors did more than recognize themselves, for the main character in every story is God. We do violence to the story if we make it only a description of the human condition. Each of these accounts contains a meeting between humans and God, and it becomes revelation for us when the story enables us also to encounter that same God. That has happened again and again, calling believing communities into existence and nourishing them, and it is because these stories have been effective, because they do bring readers into the presence of God, that believers have no choice but to affirm that this is the inspired Word of God.

THE CREATION
OF THE WORLD
Genesis 1:1–2:4a

The first words of the Bible are so widely familiar that it is tempting to assume that the only appropriate way to begin the history of salvation is with the story of the creation of the world. Our awareness that virtually every culture in the world possesses its own creation stories tends to support that assumption, but sound interpretation of the Scriptures should not leave any assumption unexamined. One ought to begin the study of Genesis by asking why we need a creation story. What do people need to know about how the world came into existence and, more specifically, what did the author of Gen. 1 clearly want us to know about it? That he was interested in purely theoretical knowledge—to satisfy his and our curiosity—is very doubtful, for stories about creation have practical meaning for daily life in other cultures. The Babylonian creation story, Enuma Elish, has a clearly political intention in its final form, for it validates the superiority of Marduk, the god of Babylon, over the older gods who had previously been primary in the city cults of Mesopotamia. It is not a solely political composition, however, for we know that in its use in the Babylonian New Year festival it helped to answer a basic human need by the assurance that time and the world could be renewed. Other creation stories that are now known to us from the cuneiform texts of ancient Mesopotamia conclude with the building of temples and provision for the maintenance of their cults, so they served to validate holy places and the status of the priests attached to those temples. But they might have significance for incidental occurrences in the lives of ordinary people as well. The procedure for curing toothaches, for example, is introduced by reciting in brief the creation of the world up to the appearance of the worm, which was considered to be the cause of dental trouble. In other cultures taking possession of an area or even building a house required recitations and rituals reenacting the creation of the world. The inauguration of a new chieftain might be called "the creation of the world." A creation story might be told for protection when a harvest was endangered, and individual characteristics or the differences between cultures would be explained by telling a story about how they began.

We ought to expect, then, that the author of Gen. 1, whom for convenience we shall call "P," had a point to make in his very careful construction of these impressive verses, and that he would not intend to leave his readers guessing as to what it was. In order that we read the chapter as intelligently as possible, asking the right kinds of questions about it, the major concern of the author ought to be identified. Certain common uses of creation stories can quickly be ruled out. There is no hint of a "political" concern here. Creation is used that way in Second Isaiah, who contrasts the creative work of Yahweh with the powerlessness of other gods (Isa. 43:1-21; 45:5-21), and in Jer. 33:17-26, which reaffirms God's promises to the descendants of David and Levi. Moreover, it is common in other cultures to connect one's possession of a given land with creation itself; but no hint of any of these concerns appears in Gen. 1.

Neither is the aim of the chapter clearly cultic, for it says nothing of the holy city, Jerusalem, or of the establishment of a temple or priesthood. It does conclude with the sanctification of the seventh day, showing that the sabbath day is of such importance to the author that he associates it with creation itself; but he does not explicitly draw the law of the sabbath from creation, as he easily could have done and as the Exodus form of the Decalogue does (Exod. 20:8-11). Could the chapter simply have been written for information, then, to satisfy the curiosity of those whose intellects may have led them to speculate about where the world came from—information that one could very easily live without? That scarcely seems to be an acceptable conclusion, for the creation stories of other cultures are not used that way, and one would be hard-pressed to find anything else in the OT that was included simply to satisfy curiosity.

Other creation stories lead up to a conclusion that immediately tells one what they are for. The structure of Gen. 1:1–2:4a would suggest that it is written to validate keeping the sabbath, and yet if that were the author's prime concern he surely would have told it plainly and explicitly, for he knows how to write in a clear and straightforward manner. These considerations draw us to the next-to-last act, however—the creation of humanity, which is told at relatively great length and with considerable elaboration (Gen. 1:26-31). Here we might logically expect to find a message directed to human beings concerning their status in the world, and that does in fact appear. Human beings have been created in the image of God, have been given dominion over the earth, and have been given all the earth's fruits and vegetables to eat. Could it be a message about diet? Surely it must be more important than that. Is it, then, an appointment to a position of great honor in the created world, as king of the world, representing God himself to all the rest of creation? So it seems to say, and so it has been interpreted, without doubt correctly. But who needs such a message? Aren't we already tempted far too much to make little kings of ourselves? Is this a word for "shy persons," who need help with their inferiority complexes? I believe that P has indicated the need for this message; the problem he intends to address presents itself in two appropriate places, near the beginning and near the end of his account.

The account of creation written by P is one of the clearest and simplest passages in the Bible, except for one verse: "The earth was without form and void, and darkness was upon the face of the deep; and the Spirit of God was moving over the face of the waters" (Gen. 1:2). These words do not fit the pattern of creation, which begins with v. 3, and it is only by extremes of exegetical ingenuity that their content can be made congruent with the rest of the chapter. Could so careful an author somehow have lost control of his material at one crucial point, at the very beginning of his account? That scarcely seems likely. I intend to suggest that this apparent anomaly in structure and content is deliberate and provides the clue to a major concern of the author that probably could not have been better expressed in any other way. The concern is what may be called "cosmic evil," that is, everything we identify as destructive and productive of pain that can in no way be considered a result of human sin. We can understand why that subject and creation are intimately related with one another; and if our preliminary estimate of the meaning of v. 2 is correct, we can also begin to understand the necessity of the promise offered near the end of the account: "You shall subdue the earth" (v. 28). But a preliminary statement of the case needs to be made here before comments on each section of the chapter are made.

The Structure of Genesis 1:1–2:4a

The style of P is serene and stately. Not only is there no trace of conflict or violence, such as may be found in many creation stories and in the echoes of Near Eastern myths elsewhere in the OT (Job 26:12-13; Ps. 74:13-14; 89:9-11; Isa. 51:9). There is really no description of divine activity, such as appears in Gen. 2:7 and many extrabiblical parallels. God creates, and there is no human analogy to that. God speaks, makes, separates, sees, and blesses, and there is no drama, not the slightest sense of tension in the way these stupendous events are recorded. All is placid and completely under control, an effect produced by the use of formulas that regularly reappear.

Each act of creation (except for the creation of humanity) is introduced by "And God said." The essence of the story is creation by fiat. The command is usually in the form of a jussive verb, not an imperative: "Let there be. . . ." "Let the waters be gathered. . . ." "Let the waters swarm with. . . ." "Let the earth bring forth. . . ." Sometimes the author adds "And God made . . ." or "And God separated . . . ," but without any description of what such divine activity would involve. Typical of the certainty of all that God wills, in keeping with creation by fiat and the use of jussives, are the formulas, "And it was so," and "God saw that it was good."

These formulas provide clues to structure, but they are combined with another structuring element, the seven-day pattern, and this combination has taxed the ingenuity of scholars. The passage may be outlined in several ways, and it is impossible to demonstrate that any one of them is the way that P had in mind. Rather, the possibility of more than one outline reveals the genius of the passage and the actual intricacy of what appears at first glance to be a simple plan, for each outline points out a different emphasis in the message. We shall not concern ourselves with theories that attempt to understand the passage as the combination of an earlier "act-narrative" with a later "word-narrative" or with other suggestions of redactorial work, for the text has an integrity as it now stands and we have enough to do in trying to understand that.

Some outlines focus on the question of why eight works of creation are presented in a six-day scheme, and suggest various explanations of that; others reject the focus on six days and use the seven-day pattern as the key to the structure of the whole. Let us consider some of the patterns that have been detected.

Those who focus on the six days of creation usually divide them into two corresponding parts. The first three days produce an ordered structure, or focus on spaces; the final three speak of "peopling," providing residents of the various regions of the cosmos.

Day One: Light	Day Four: The Luminaries
Day Two: Sea and Atmosphere	Day Five: Fish and Birds
Day Three: Dry Land	Day Six: Land animals, People,
Vegetation	Vegetation given as
	food

Fault has been found with some of the parallels in this pattern, but the general correspondence at least is clear. A chiastic relationship has also been noted in the six-day structure.

Days One-Three:	Heavens	Heavens	Earth
Days Four-Six:	Heavens	Earth	Earth

When the six days of creation are outlined in this way, then a parallel is noted between Gen. 1:1 as introduction and 2:1-3 as conclusion, but the outline does not account for 1:2.

The seven-day outline is based on the observation that days two and three provide space for living things, and days five and six refer to the population of those spaces. The other three days are concerned with time: the separation of light from darkness to produce the elementary division of time (the day) on day one, the provision of heavenly bodies to mark off seasons, days, and years on day four, and the sanctification of the sabbath on day seven. So creation is the provision of time and space for living things.

Day One: Time—The Day
Day Two: Space—Sea and Atmosphere
Day Three: Space—Dry Land
Day Four: Time—The Luminaries
Day Five: Population—Fish and Birds
Day Six: Population—Land Animals, People
Day Seven: Time—The Sabbath

The seven-day pattern also finds a conclusion corresponding to Gen. 1:1, but it is 2:4a: "These are the generations of the heavens and the earth when they were created." Once again, Gen. 1:2 stands by itself.

Could this learned and skillful author have been reworking older, mythological accounts of creation and have simply been unsuccessful in completely "demythologizing" the old stories that spoke of preexisting, formless matter or of chaotic powers that needed to be overcome? Some scholars have drawn this conclusion, but it seems unlikely on the face of it that such a careful piece of work could contain one such blatant inadvertency, and at the very beginning. The presence of 1:2 and its wording must be deliberate, and so we must ask why P chose to say this.

As the commentary on this passage explains, although the theology of P allows for only one source of all things and insists as firmly as possible that the source is good and produced a cosmos that is wholly good, the author realistically enough could not completely deny the existence of certain evils in the world that cannot be blamed on human sin. In his Creation account the author is not concerned about sin at all; that will come later. But he knows that conditions exist that are inappropriate for God's purposes, for they do not support life but are contrary to all that he believes God would pronounce "good." The author cannot ascribe something inadequate, not life-sustaining and enriching, to the work of God. Neither will his theology permit him to speak of some chaotic reality that exists apart from and over against the being and will of God. Yet he is aware of some such threat, of which he must somehow take account; and that, I suggest, accounts for the appearance in this passage of simple and straightforward prose of one bit of extremely difficult, ambiguous syntax that does not fit the pattern. It will be argued in the Commentary that Gen. 1:1-2 does not fit the pattern because the subject matter does not fit any rational account of creation, and that P was wise enough to recognize that there is no better way for a human being to acknowledge it.

Setting and Genre

Since the 19th cent., when most biblical scholars accepted the division of the Pentateuch into several written sources, the Creation account has been considered to be a classic example of the work of the Priestly source (P). No discussion of source criticism (formerly called the documentary hypothesis) can be offered here; it is readily available elsewhere. The supposed priestly character of this passage and its suggested date and location are relevant for one's interpretation of its theology, however. The Priestly source has usually been dated after the fall of Jerusalem to the Babylonians in 587 B.C., between the middle of the 6th cent. and the middle of the 5th cent. It is thought to reflect a setting in the Babylonian exile, and some scholars have written on the significance of the exilic setting for the message of P. Other scholars still try to claim all of the Pentateuch for Moses, which would make the Creation account a message for Israel in the time of the wilderness wanderings, and others point to evidence that it originated during the Monarchy. But the exilic setting of this source has better support than any other. The introduction to the message of this passage will thus be based on its supposed exilic setting, but will be developed in such a way that it should not lose its validity if another date is assigned it.

If Gen. 1:1-2:4a was written in exile, we can easily understand why creation was not used for the purposes that are customary in other cultures. There was no point in associating Jerusalem or its temple, the priestly establishment, kingship, or the occupation of the land with a creation story, for all of this had been lost. Anything P had to say about creation was addressed to a downtrodden people who had lost everything, victims of their own sins and the sins of others, at the mercy of the powers of this world. If this describes the initial readers of P's Creation account, then this passage must be seen as a bold challenge to them to believe something that was not visible in the world around them and in no way confirmed by their recent experiences. The creation message asserts that the whole world belongs to God, that it is good, and that he is in charge. It concludes with the assurance that they are worth something, after all, despite having lost everything. And the commission given to humanity, to subdue the earth, speaks of the essential conditions for life to continue and to be more than a miserable existence for those exiles. In their circumstances was a great deal that needed to be subdued! The author supports these bold claims with a series of calm affirmations concerning the order, regularity, and predictability of the natural world, much of which his readers could verify for themselves. We must admit that he does overstate the case, for this world is not as neat as he claims. His world, in which everything is pronounced to be "very good," with everything in order and humanity living under God's full blessing, is a world that has never yet existed in real time. Such overstatements are sometimes needed in desperate cases, however, in order to get across a message that is hard to believe. The exile in Babylonia is a classic example of such a time, but it is not the only occasion in history when people have had to face a world that seems to be going out of control. In any such time, the challenge of P's Creation account is to ask whether we can believe that *this* is the world created by the God of Gen. 1.

The form critical analysis of the OT usually identifies the literary genre of a passage by comparing it with a group of similar texts, noting the reappearance of formulaic speech and parallels in structure. This means that any statement about the genre of Gen. 1:1–2:4a can only be very tentative, for it has no true parallels. The form of Gen. 2:4b-25 is distinctly different, as are the other creation materials in the Psalms, Second Isaiah, and Prov. 8. Gen. 1:1–2:4a is clearly not a "creation myth," for when we compare it with the abundant examples of the genre known from other cultures it is evident that it has neither the form nor the function of true myth. It has been called "poetry," sometimes with reference to its repetitive features, sometimes as a vague way of saying its details should not be taken literally; but this is not good form criticism, for the passage is prose, as a comparison with the true creation poetry of Ps. 104 and Prov.

8:22-31 will show. It has recently been designated a *report*, that is, a genre that describes events for the sake of communication. That term seems a little misleading when we think about the form and contents of Gen. 1:1–2:4a, but it is certainly more adequate than earlier suggestions; and when coupled with another suggestion, that this is priestly doctrine, we may be on the right track, recognizing that this is a unique form produced essentially for teaching purposes. Evidence for the priestly character of the instruction will be noted along the way, but can be summed up here by calling attention to the strong interest in separation (of clean from unclean, holy from profane), in time (associated with the importance of the calendar), and most obviously in the seven-day week, climaxing in the sabbath day.

The Beginning of Creation (1:1-2)

The Bible begins with a statement unlike that which can be found in any other known creation story (including the one in Gen. 2:4b-25). It speaks of a "beginning," that is, a time prior to which one cannot go. Scripture has nothing to say about what preceded the creation of the world, not even any statement about the prior existence of God. That is clearly none of our business, even if it were possible to conceive it. The difficulty of thinking about so absolute a beginning as this is reflected in the problem of understanding exactly what 1:1-2 are saying. The verses may be translated three possible ways: (1) the traditional way, with v. 1 an independent sentence; (2) taking v. 1 as a dependent clause with v. 2 the independent clause: "At the beginning of God's creating the heavens and the earth, the earth was waste and void . . ."; (3) taking v. 1 as a dependent clause with v. 3 as the independent clause and v. 2 as a parenthesis: "At the beginning of God's creating the heavens and the earth—the earth being waste and void . . . —God said, 'Let there be light.'" The complex discussion of the lexical, grammatical, syntactical, comparative, and stylistic factors involved cannot be repeated here, since despite the volume of research done on the subject, no decisive argument has yet been produced. Option 3 seems to be the weakest, however. Studies of the structure of the passage, already alluded to, agree that v. 3 ought to stand by itself, as the first act of creation, so vv. 1-2 should not be dependent on it. Also, combining vv. 1-3 into one, long, rambling sentence produces a construction so completely different from the simple, straightforward sentences comprising the rest of the passage that it is difficult to believe P could have strayed so far from his controlled presentation as to produce that "syntactic monster" (as one scholar called it) as his intro-

17

ductory words. Options 1 and 2 seem to be almost equally possible, according to what we know.

Options 1 and 2 both raise questions about the nature of the creative act. Neither explicitly states that God created the world out of nothing, although v. 1, taken as an independent sentence, can be argued as supporting that (as has been done for centuries). But if v. 1 states that the heavens and earth (i.e., the cosmos) were created out of nothing, what is v. 2 talking about? The most common answer has been that this is the first stage; God initially created the formless materials of the cosmos, then proceeded to shape something of them. But many scholars have found this to be an unsatisfactory explanation. Those who claim that v. 1 is a temporal clause, dependent on v. 2, conclude that it is therefore impossible to deduce creation out of nothing from these verses, for they simply tell us how God began to create order out of preexisting chaos. It may be asked whether that is necessarily so. "At the beginning of God's creating the heavens and the earth the earth was waste and void . . ." might be speaking of beginning as the first creative step, the production of formless matter. But the question that intrudes itself is why P, who is so clear and so careful to make himself understood everywhere else, leaves us with the apparently unresolvable dilemma presented by these first two verses. After discussion of the key terms, an answer will be offered, appealing to the subject matter as the reason for the problem.

The Hebrew word *reshith* (beginning) is used fifty times in the Bible, but in only one place that is a good parallel to this passage: Isa. 46:10, which seems to speak of an absolute end and an absolute beginning. All other beginnings occur in the midst of history, which means the use of the word elsewhere cannot provide us certain knowledge about what P may have meant by it in Gen. 1:1. A similar problem of uniqueness is associated with *bara'* ("create"). Only God is the subject of this verb in Hebrew, and so it is restricted in meaning to divine activity, unlike our use of the English word "create." This means there are no true analogies to the expression "God created" to be found within human experience. Hence the first three words of the Bible, "In the beginning God created" (or "When God began to create") must be most accurately taken as celebrating a mystery. The author insists on giving God complete priority, exclusive initiative, and sole instrumentality as he ponders our existence and this place in which we exist. As the first word denotes something unique that can never be repeated and the second word ("create") denotes something exclusive, which only God can do, the concluding words of the verse are comprehensive; "heavens and earth" is the typical Hebrew way of speaking of the cosmos, the entire created universe. Some early interpreters, understanding this, then insisted that the cosmos was created in an instant, in spite of the seven-day pattern that follows; but that surely was not P's idea, for time is a crucial element in his scheme. A better way to understand the intention of this verse is to take it as a true introduction, a heading that sums up the gist of the whole passage.

Logically, then, one would think v. 3 should come next, but interrupting the smooth flow of divine activity is a series of three difficult clauses. "The earth was *tohu wabohu*" uses a pair of words that occur together in two other places (Isa. 34:11; Jer. 4:23), denoting an utterly desolate place. The familiar "waste and void" (or as an alternative, "desolate and empty") are English terms that convey reasonably well the meaning and the feeling of these words. Immediately P's attention turns to earth, for he is reporting God's preparation of a place for human beings to live and anything that does not directly impinge on human life does not interest him greatly. The second clause uses two more words expressive of disorder and threat to life, "darkness" and "the deep." The symbolic value of darkness and light is so obvious to everyone that it scarcely needs to be explained. Throughout the Bible darkness represents evil and the threat to life, while life represents good, life itself, and even God himself (John 1:4-9). The word translated "deep" *(tehom)* has for a long time been associated with Tiamat, the antagonist of Marduk in the Babylonian creation epic; Tiamat represents disorder, and her body is used by Marduk as the raw materials from which to create the world. But this association should not be overemphasized, for although the two words may be related, there is no similarity of thought. *Tehom* in the OT simply represents the cosmic ocean and in no case is it an enemy that God defeats, nor does it furnish the materials from which he creates anything. It is an exact parallel to the "waters" in the third clause of this verse.

The third clause in Gen. 1:2 is one of the most difficult in the entire passage, because of the ambiguity of one word and the rareness of another. The word *ruah,* traditionally translated "spirit," can also mean wind or breath. And the Hebrew root of *merahephet* occurs in only two other places, Deut. 32:11 and Jer. 23:9, where it is used of an eagle that spreads out its wings over its nest and of the wavering movements of a drunken man. Now the issue is this: Is this third clause a continuation of the description of chaotic conditions found in the first two, does it describe the presence of God even in the midst of chaos, or is it a direct introduction to the creative word of Gen. 1:3? For those who believe the first option makes the most sense, *ruah* must be translated "wind," and since *elohim* (God) can sometimes be used as a superlative adjective, something like "mighty wind" is a possible translation. However, the two uses of *merahephet* elsewhere do not suggest the kind of movement that would be expected of a mighty wind; and it would seem an odd choice of terms for P, who uses the word *elohim* of the Creator so prominently in verse after verse, to use the same word as an ordinary adjective here. Spirit or breath of God thus seem to be more likely renderings; and if we can draw any conclusions about the kind of movement described from the other two occurrences of *merahephet,* it is likely to be something like hovering, as a bird does. It does not mean "brooding," so does not denote some process by which the cosmos was produced out of chaos, as some scholars have suggested. Others have noted the relationship between breath and the spoken word in Hebrew usage elsewhere in the OT and have suggested this is a direct introduction to "And God said."

That this clause represents an action of God contrary to the conditions denoted in the first two clauses is supported by the observation that creation deals with each element of those clauses. Form takes the place of shapelessness and populations fill the empty spaces. Light is created and the realm of darkness is limited. Boundaries are set for the deep so that the dry land may be inhabited. But if we were to take the third clause as an additional chaotic element, a mighty wind raging over the surface of the waters, then we would be left with a storm that is never stilled, never alluded to in the work of creation. The *ruah elohim* must be either Spirit of God or breath of God, an introduction to v. 3.

We have seen that v. 2 does not fit any of the various outlines of the passages that have been proposed, and the exact relationship between v. 1 and v. 2 cannot be established with certainty. And yet the rest of the passage is remarkably regular, unusually simple in its choice of words and its syntax. I suggest that the reason for this peculiarity is to be found in the subject. The verse does not fit because the subject does not fit. The theology of P emphasizes without qualification that God is the only source of anything that exists and that the will of God is for good, and only for good. Yet this author is no sheltered person who can imagine that the world of the present is perfect; he is realistic enough and honest enough to acknowledge that there is a "shadow" to God's good creative work. But how can one speak or think of that? To say that chaos existed before God began to create would be to acknowledge that something negative, contrary to God, existed alongside God in the beginning, and P will not do that. To say that God created the negative, life-threatening forces in the cosmos is completely contrary to P's theology. Yet he is aware of conditions in the material world that are inadequate for God's purposes since they do not support life—they exist or at least threaten to appear. That becomes evident in P's account of the Flood, when "all the fountains of the great deep burst forth, and the windows of the heavens were opened" (7:11; cf. 8:2). That is, P knows that disorder, the threat of annihilation of God's good creation, may reappear in this world. He remains optimistic, in his account of the Flood as in his telling of creation, for in the covenant with Noah God promises never again to destroy the earth with a flood (9:9-15). But P knows he cannot ignore the threat. He must assure us that God deals with it.

This is P's wise way of acknowledging the problem of evil, the evils that afflict human existence but cannot be attributed to human sin. To whom can they be attributed, then? Not to God, P insists. They do not fit the structure of the creation of the universe because they are what God did not will. They stand awkwardly between the announcement of the creation of a complete cosmos (1:1) and the description of how God produced order and life. As Karl Barth commented, these words represent "the world which according to His revelation was negated, rejected, ignored and left behind in His actual creation" (*Church Dogmatics*, III/1, 108). The Priestly writer recognizes that nothing positive can be said about cosmic evil; it will not fit any theology that confesses an omnipotent, righteous God, and yet it continues to threaten. As P's accounts of creation and the Flood show us, faith in the omnipotent, righteous God enables us to push the threat far out to the very fringes of existence, and yet it will not completely disappear. Since that is true, and since it is very likely that this passage was produced under circumstances where all that was good in the lives of writer and readers had been challenged and lost, it is a remarkable testimony, for it refuses to speak of any conflict. God is completely in charge, and all proceeds serenely.

Day One—Light (1:3-5)

Although P does not speak explicitly of creation out of nothing, the events of day one come very close to it. Light does appear to be a substance that can exist without a physical source, since the sun will not be created until the fourth day; but even if v. 2 is interpreted as a description of the material from which God made the world, it is

21

hard to imagine any relationship between that stuff and light, and nowhere does the OT suggest such a relationship. The absolute control that God possesses over the cosmos is suggested by his first creative act, which is merely two words (in Hebrew), "Let there be light," with an instantaneous result. The word is power in itself, for there is no one to hear it and respond. It is no command, but is an effective act in itself.

Why is light the first thing created, even before light sources? The importance of life in this passage might make us think of "scientific" reasons, that light is essential for life, but that is probably not as important as two other factors. Although P did not have our knowledge of creatures that can live in total darkness, in his culture it was probably thought that such beings did exist. A more important reason is the symbolic value of light, representing the presence of God himself in the world and portending the appearance of life. But even more significant for P is the association of light with time. In the division of light from darkness the day, which was the basic unit of time for the Jews, came into existence. Time itself was a result of God's first creative word. One of the symbols of formlessness, disorder, and the threat to life—darkness—was thus brought under control on the first day. Notice that it was not destroyed, nor was it transformed; God does not call the darkness good. It was no substance that preexisted light, but was only the nonexistence of light. Although darkness is given a name and a time, it is not created. Light stands over against it, and the domain of darkness is restricted. Light is called "good" by its Creator, meaning it is pleasing because it is *suitable for God's intended purpose.* If we have correctly understood the setting in which this passage was written, then the appearance of the word "good" seven times is one of several ways by which P intends to offer a revelation of God's true intentions in order to contradict what experience has taught them.

The separation of light from darkness is God's first act of ordering, one of P's favorite themes. Naming is no insignificant thing in the culture of P's time, for it indicates knowledge of the true nature of the thing named and control over it. So God affirms his sovereignty over both light and darkness by giving them names, Day and Night. And with this, time begins. Light is followed by darkness (the evening) but in its due time returns (the morning), and so the day is defined. All efforts to redefine the day of Gen. 1 as equivalent to geological periods must stumble over P's unequivocal definition of it in terms of successive periods of light and darkness. Time as human beings experience it has begun.

Day Two—The Sky (1:6-8)

The effect of God's second creative act is to produce what we would call the atmosphere. He creates the "firmament," our translation of a Hebrew word that literally means something firm, a dome that produces an air bubble with water above and water below. This reflects the commonsense cosmology of the ancient world; since water falls from the heavens, a great body of water must be located up there somewhere, and some rigid structure to support it. Pre-19th cent. interpreters seem to have been able to accept the creation of light prior to the sun without much trouble; but they did struggle with this idea of waters above the sky, since it did not correspond with what the science of their day taught about the atmosphere. Martin Luther confessed, "Here I, therefore, take my reason captive and subscribe to the Word even though I do not understand it" (*Lectures on Genesis Chapters 1-5*, 26), but then went on discussing it for another two pages. He commended to his listeners Jerome, "who maintains complete silence on these topics," but still could not resist further efforts to understand it in terms of the "modern science" of his day—efforts that now look ludicrous to us. But in our own time the same thing happens, only more blatantly, in the name of "creation science." People think they are doing something of value by finding ways to correlate Gen. 1 with 20th-cent. science, efforts that will probably look as primitive and useless to people four hundred years from now as Luther's do to us. We would do well to heed the wisdom of John Calvin, who wrote, "He who would learn astronomy, and other recondite arts, let him go elsewhere," and then followed his own advice.

This time the creative act involves both speaking (v. 6) and making (v. 7). This double description has led scholars to postulate a two-stage process in the formation of the passage, involving an earlier "deed account" that was reworked by P, adding his "word account." Recent studies have begun to question this, however, since it has not been possible to make any neat separation of the two narratives, and there is no evidence elsewhere in the OT to suggest that Israel would have made a distinction between God's word and God's act. The formula, "and it was so," can be used between an announcement and the event itself, as in vv. 11, 15, 24; Judg. 6:38; and 2 Kgs. 7:20; or as a summary, as in Gen. 1:7, 9; and 2 Kgs. 15:12. The firmament is named "Heaven." This word in the OT normally means simply the sky, and not the place where the righteous go when they die. Occasionally God is said to dwell in heaven (Ps. 2:4), but it was understood that God cannot be limited to heaven (1 Kgs. 8:27). As for human beings, Elijah did go up to heaven in a chariot of fire (2 Kgs. 2:11), but ordinarily that is no place for people (Isa. 14:12-15). The concept of a supernatural heaven, a place somewhere above the dome of the sky where God and the blessed dead dwell, developed in Judaism during the intertestamental period.

Day Three—Land and Vegetation (1:9-13)

Days two and three are related in that their results are the three realms—atmosphere, sea, and land—that will be populated in days five and six. The first act of day three does not bring anything new into being, but is another work of separation, producing a body of water called "Sea" and dry land called "Earth," using the same word that appeared in Gen. 1:1 and 2. This setting of boundaries for the sea is another of P's affirmations concerning God's control of the cosmic threat. God is praised for the same activity in more picturesque, poetic language in Job 38:8-11; Ps. 104:5-9; and Prov. 8:29. The creation of plant life, as a second creative act on this day, is described in a new way. God instructs the earth, it seems, to bring forth vegetation, and it happens. Plants are created on the same day as the land, indicating that P thought of the earth's vegetation as a part of God's provision of space in which the land animals will live. We think of both plants and animals as alive, distinguishing them by calling the former inanimate and the latter animate; but it appears the OT does not attribute life to the plant world, since the blessing that God bestows on all living creatures created on days five and six is missing here. The author shows a type of scientific interest in vegetation, however, in his classification of plants into two types, those that bear seeds and those that bear fruit. Science began in this way, in antiquity, by the observation of similarities and the making of lists. This work of classification of things in nature was one of the Priestly interests, as the lists in passages such as Lev. 11 and 13 reveal. But there is a pastoral concern revealed here also, in the repeated emphasis, "according to its kind." The reader is reminded that God has put regularity and predictability into his world. If one plants a lettuce seed, a lettuce plant will come up, not an onion. This is visible evidence that God has created a world of order and dependability that P can set over against the experiences to the contrary that his readers may have suffered.

Day Four—Heavenly Bodies (1:14-19)

A significant amount of space is now devoted to the creation of sun and moon, in order to explain at length what they are for. The apparent discrepancy with reality, having light exist and day and night come and go for three days before the sun comes into existence, is not so difficult a problem as it might seem. We have already noted that light is obviously considered to be a substance with an existence of its own. Evidently the alternation of light and darkness was, at least for the author's present purposes, not considered to be absolutely dependent on the movements of the sun. It is generally agreed that the sun and moon do not make their appearance until the fourth day for polemic reasons. The heavenly bodies were worshipped in every religion but that of Israel, and the sun, moon, and Venus were often major deities in the pantheon. For P they are certainly not deities, nor are they even essential for the existence of a habitable world—a position likely to be taken only when one is fighting against extravagant claims for those luminaries. He does not even mention their common Hebrew names, *shamash* and *yareah,* for these were divine names in the neighboring cultures. Furthermore, their value is strictly defined, and it is limited to keeping time. The calendar was very important to the priesthood, since it was the priests' responsibility to mark off the holy times and keep them sacred, and that interest appears here. Note especially the "seasons," which are mentioned in v. 14. These are not spring, fall, and the like, but the "appointed times," such as the great pilgrimage feasts (Passover, Weeks, and Booths) and other holy days. In some early Jewish traditions New Year's Day always came on Wednesday, because that was when the calendar began, with the appearance of these celestial timekeepers. In P's structuring of creation, time began with the creation of light on day one, space for life was provided on days two and three, and time-keeping began in the middle of the week.

Now God sets about to provide the populations that are to enjoy his time and space.

Day Five—Fish and Birds (1:20-23)

God now populates the three regions that were produced on days two and three. Earlier interpreters puzzled over the implication of v. 20 that birds as well as fish were produced from the waters, although the Hebrew is by no means explicit about that. With our present knowledge of evolution we might find it not strange at all, but neither the science of earlier centuries nor that of today has anything to do with P's arrangement of things. On day two the atmosphere was produced because of the creation of the firmament, so the waters below (the realm of fish) and the region under the firmament (the realm of birds) were the work of the same day. Now the creation of living beings corresponds to that earlier division of regions, and the dry land, which appeared on the third day, will be populated on the sixth.

God makes use of both earth and water in bringing forth life: "Let the earth put forth vegetation" (v. 11); "Let the waters bring forth swarms of living creatures" (v. 20); "Let the earth bring forth living creatures" (v. 24). This scarcely suggests that P attributed life-giving powers to "Mother Earth" ("Mother Sea"?), for the word *bara* ("create") reappears for the first time since v. 1 in connection with fish and birds, and will be used of human beings (for some reason it is not used of land animals, but that is probably not significant). The intimate relationship of animate beings to their proper domains (sea or land) is indicated here, but God remains the sole creator.

God's mastery over everything is nicely alluded to, without any special emphasis, in the reference to his creation of the *tanninim,* "great sea monsters." This word is sometimes used of serpents (Exod. 7:9; Deut. 32:33), but usually designates a large sea creature, with mythological overtones that are to be seen in Job 7:12; Ps. 74:13; Isa. 27:1; 51:9; Ezek. 29:3; 32:2. The word is used along with Leviathan and Rahab, two other terms for sea monsters. In the texts just mentioned the *tannin* is defeated by God, reflecting the conflict motif so common in other cultures; but in Gen. 1 it is just another of God's creatures. In Ps. 148:7, which obviously shares P's theology, they are called upon to praise God, and in Ps. 104:26 God is said to have made Leviathan to "sport" in the sea. As one scholar has said, no longer are the great sea monsters enemies of God; they are his playthings. One more blow has been struck by P against that fear of chaos that was represented in myth by stories of monsters.

Animate beings receive a blessing, unlike anything previously created, and the content of the blessing is the ability to reproduce themselves—that is, the ability for an individual to pass on life directly to another being like itself. Before we become too impressed by the special place given to human beings in God's world, we ought to contemplate this significant element that we have in common with the birds and the fish, in the sight of God. They also are honored by him, as he bestows upon them a blessing.

Day Six—Animals and Human Beings (1:24-31)

On the sixth day all the land creatures are made, including human beings, as a way of acknowledging what people have in common with the other animals. No blessing is given until it can include the relationship between human beings and the other creatures, and the provisions for food are addressed to all at the end of the section. People, however, differ from the other inhabitants of the earth in two ways: they are created in the image of God, and they are to rule over all other animate beings. The tendency of P to classify reappears in his threefold description of land animals. He seems to be satisfied with two categories of large animals, wild (beasts of the earth) and domesticated (cattle), and puts all the small animals into one big category, "creeping things." That a much more elaborate system based on careful observation could be devised by Israelite thinkers is revealed by examples such as Lev. 11.

Innumerable pages have been written on the statement, "Let us make man in our image, after our likeness," but space does not permit a review of that lengthy and inconclusive discussion. We shall present these verses in a way different from what most interpreters have used, viewing them as P's interpretation of the earlier account of the creation of humanity in Gen. 2–3, attributed to the Yahwistic source (J). The author of ch. 1 surely knew the J source, and may even have been responsible for combining his own work with chs. 2–3. Gen. 1:26-31 contains many indications of P's knowledge of J and of its influence on the way he presents the creation of human beings. But the theology of P is very different from that of J at this point, so the same ideas are used in different ways. This section will conclude with a suggested reason for the difference in their messages.

"Let *us* make . . . in *our* image after (or "according to") *our* likeness": The divine plural also occurs in Gen. 3:22: "the man has become like one of us, knowing good and evil." There is no support in the OT for most of the proposed explanations: the royal "we," the deliberative "we," the plural of fullness, or an indication of a plurality of persons in the Godhead. Although it can be claimed that each supplied a good interpretation of 1:26, none of these explanations makes much sense in 3:22, which speaks of "one of us." The only theory that uses the language of the OT itself is that which claims God is here addressing the heavenly court, as in Isa. 6:8. That God was believed to consult with spiritual creatures in heaven is revealed by the scenes described in 1 Kgs. 22:19-22 and Job 1:6–2:6. Hence the consultative "we" has support from other texts, and it fits both Gen. 1:26-27 and 3:22, on the assumption that Israel believed there were creatures in the heavenly realm ("the host of heaven," 1 Kgs. 22:19) whose identity had something in common both with God and with human beings. The familiar objection that angels could not have participated in creation is a theological judgment about what is possible in heaven. Consultation is documented in the texts just mentioned, and God's discussion concerning the creation of humanity may have been thought by P and J to have involved nothing more than that.

The new creature is called *adam*, a term for which we have no adequate English equivalent. Eventually it becomes the name of the first man (Gen. 4:1); but here it is not a name, nor a reference to one individual, nor a designation of maleness (1:27). Usually I render the term "human beings"; sometimes for the sake of brevity I convert the adjective "human" into a noun. Unlike Gen. 2, which speaks of the creation of two people, this passage contains no reference to a single pair but seems to be thinking of the human population of the earth.

"In our image, after (or "according to") our likeness": P provides few clues as to what he intended by this expression, leaving most interpreters to the free play of their imaginations; as a result, most explanations have appealed to philosophical, psychological, and theological concepts of humanity. What can exegesis teach us? We have already noted that J comments on a likeness between humanity and God in 3:22 (identified as the knowledge of good and evil), but believes that this likeness is not a part of God's original intention. Such an irregularity is not even alluded to by P. He may have been influenced in his choice of words by the fact that in 2:7 God actually makes a physical image, from the dust of the earth. He was certainly also influenced by Ezekiel's description of his vision of God, in which he saw, seated on a throne, "a likeness as of the appearance of a man" (Ezek. 1:26 author's translation; cf. vv. 27, 28). No one can see God, according to Israelite thought, but the closest one can get is a vision of a form something like the human shape. Poetically, of course, the Israelites could speak of the mouth of the LORD, the arm of the LORD, and the like; but they knew better than to take those anthropomorphisms literally. The authors of Ezek. 1 and Gen. 1, however (both exilic in date), became a little bolder in speaking of an almost physical resemblance, but they were very careful not to go too far. It is likely that what P means by this similarity is that communication and understanding between God and humanity are possible, as they are *not* possible between totally different species of creatures. Recall how he emphasizes the continuity and predictability of each living thing, which reproduces "according to its kind." His use of two different terms ("image" and "likeness") in a similar way suggests that he cautiously speaks of a certain continuity between the Creator and this creature, and he may have dared to use such terms because of the precedents already established by Gen. 2:7 and Ezek. 1:26. The continuity indicated by "image," rather than "kind," appears to include both communication and responsibility, as the next clause suggests.

"Let them have dominion": The special place of human beings on earth may have been suggested to P by Gen. 2:19-20, which speaks of God creating all the animals in the search for a companion for the man, and of the latter's contribution of their names. Naming indicates knowledge and power, as we have noted, so we find both writers saying something similar about human rule over all the animate world.

> So God created *adam* in his own image,
> in the image of God he created him;
> male and female he created them.

If one assumed that P was using strict parallelism here to define what he meant by "image" there could be no doubt; it is our existence as male and female that corresponds to the image of God in humanity. Karl Barth and Dietrich Bonhoeffer followed this lead in their interpretations; but what Barth, especially, made of it is also dependent on his understanding of the divine plural as indicating "a concert of mind and action in the divine being itself," for which there is no support in the OT. He concluded that "I" and "Thou" in God are related by analogy to male and female in *adam*. If we are not convinced that the OT speaks of multiple persons in the Godhead, what can the appearance of male and female here mean? Certainly fish, birds, and land animals were also made male and female, since they were ordered to be fruitful and multiply; so male and female does not distinguish *adam* from the animals. That makes the effort to identify the image of God with our existence as male and female, even by analogy, rather doubtful. I suggest that the prominence of human sexuality in P's account of creation is another example of the influence of ch. 2, in which the creation of *adam* as male and female is narrated with considerable detail and brought to a dramatic conclusion in vv. 23-25. Our existence as male and female is so important in J's story that probably P did not feel it could be left out of his compact account, and he associated it with the image of God because of the prominence of God's act of fashioning both man and woman in ch. 2. All he needed to say about the sexuality of the animals was to speak of reproduction; but the significance of our existence as male and female for the very identity of *adam* had already been developed by J, and P also acknowledges it by alluding to it in the impressive, rhythmic clauses of v. 27.

"And God blessed them, and God said to them. . . .": The first part of the blessing shows what people have in common with the other animals; indeed, P has compacted his account by omitting these words from his description of the appearance of land creatures. The distinctiveness of *adam* is now said to be his primacy over all else: "Fill the earth and subdue it; and have dominion" over all other creatures. We have already commented on the story of the creation of animals in ch. 2 as background for the promise of dominion. The whole blessing may be P's way of acknowledging the reality of the world reflected in the curses of 3:14-19, however, since reproducing and subduing are the main subjects in both places. We understand the reference to subduing in ch. 3, for it describes the world we know; but what is there to subdue in ch. 1? Everything is under control as a result of the work of God. Once again, the answer may be found by considering this to be P's reflections on J's Creation story, in this case, on the nature of the real world that appears in the curses of ch. 3. For the most part P wishes to keep that nature out of sight, except for 1:2 and here. But the truth is that the real earth must be subdued if people are to survive. The weather, hostile animals, and infertile soil threaten life and must be struggled against, something the present triumphs of technology may lead us to forget. We live in a world that technology has subdued with such devastating effects, in some cases, that we now find the words of v. 28 to be somewhat of an embarrassment. Some have blamed all of our current environmental ills on these words; but that is surely a historical mistake, for people's real motives for ecological irresponsibility have seldom been the desire to take Scripture seriously. Some have appealed to Gen. 1:28 when challenged, but such arguments tend to be after the fact. If we can imagine what it was like to live in the pretechnological world, where frail human beings were vulnerable to a terrifying array of natural forces, we may see that for people of that time "subdue" was not too strong a term, as the words of Gen. 3:17-19 remind us. Martin Luther, for example, could not in his time take "dominion" as seriously as we can, commenting, "we retain the name and word 'dominion' as a bare title, but the substance itself has been almost entirely lost."

"I have given you every plant": The parallels between ch. 1 and chs. 2–3 continue with the question of diet. What the first man may eat is a crucial issue in 2:16-17 and its unfortunate sequel in ch. 3. In both Creation accounts humanity is given a vegetarian diet, but P does not say anything of a forbidden tree. In contrast he says human beings are to have every plant and every tree, deliberately omitting the issue of the tree of knowledge because he has no intention of retelling the story of human rebellion. He has a different purpose, which we will soon be ready to sum up.

"And God saw everything that he had made, and behold, it was very good": No rebellion here. No imperfection. God is pleased with everything he sees. This is the ideal world—a world P and his readers had never experienced. But if our reading of the chapter has been correct, this is not daydreaming or idle, hypothetical speculation about how the world may have begun. It is a message for people who need some help in their effort to continue to believe in the sovereignty of God—people whose lives thus far have provided little evidence that human beings have value in the sight of God.

Day Seven—Rest (2:1-4a)

Although P does not use the word "sabbath" here, the importance of that day is made clear by his treatment of the seventh day of creation. Previously, living creatures have been blessed; now a period of time receives a blessing, and it is "hallowed," made a holy time, set apart from the other days of the week that provide time for ordinary human activities, and made God's own possession. But P does not find it appropriate to add the sabbath commandment itself to his Creation account. The first explicit reference in the Bible to the keeping of the sabbath day is in Exod. 16:23, and the sabbath commandment is associated with creation in the Exodus version of the Decalogue (Exod. 20:8-11). Here the seventh day serves primarily as the final proof of the sovereignty of God over the entire cosmos. He has finished his creative work; there is no need for continuous activity or vigilance, for all is stable, functioning properly, dependable, and at peace.

It is not certain whether the first part of Gen. 2:4 should be taken as the conclusion of P's Creation account or the beginning of the J story. The term *toledot* ("generations") is a favorite of P, but elsewhere it always appears in the heading of a genealogy (as in Gen. 5:1). There is no genealogy here, either preceding or following. Those who consider 2:4a to be the conclusion of P's account note that it corresponds well with 1:1.

The Relationship between the Two Accounts of Creation

Genesis 2:4 makes the transition between two presentations of how the world began, each with its special emphasis on the place of humanity in the world God made. The J story (Gen. 2–3), clearly the earlier, takes a very realistic, hence pessimistic view of human responsibility, with creation followed immediately by a story in which the human desire to "be like gods" provides the explanation of the perennial misery that afflicts human life on earth. But P, with full knowledge of this story, has reflected on it and has taken a boldly different view. He affirms that it was God's decision to make *adam* like him, and no shadow falls on humanity as the divinely appointed king of the world. How could he be so optimistic?

Compare the circumstances thought to lie behind these two passages. The J source is ascribed to the early years of the Monarchy, perhaps in the time of Solomon or shortly after. If this dating is correct (and not everyone agrees it is), then Gen. 2–3 was produced during a time of national success, but perhaps near to or during the reactions to Solomon that led to the division of the monarchy into two kingdoms. The message of Gen. 2–3 would be very appropriate for such a time, since it presents a realistic picture of divinely-given potential, temptations, and the devastating effects of becoming one's own god. If Gen. 1 is correctly dated in the Babylonian exile, then it was written in a time when all was lost, when the effects of sin needed not to be pointed out to anyone, but when the issue was whether their God could be depended on for anything and whether human life has any value. Genesis 1 presents resoundingly bold, unequivocal affirmation that has no time for qualifications, just as we may overstate our case precisely when it is difficult to believe. P had no need to talk of temptation and rebellion, for his readers knew enough about that. It was time for encouragement.

Whether P himself or a later redactor combined the two Creation accounts remains open to debate. Whoever it was knew better than to expurgate or revise either version, recognizing that both are needed in their appropriate times. The interpretation of the two messages that has just been offered does not depend for its validity on the dating of the two sources. Such circumstances reoccur. The sober presentation of J is needed again, whenever life seems firmly under human control, as is the message of P, when the world seems to have gone completely out of control. A Hasidic teacher, Rabbi Bunam, summed up the need for both messages in this saying, "A man should carry two stones in his pocket. On one should be inscribed, 'I am but dust and ashes.' On the other, 'For my sake was the world created.' And he should use each stone as he needs it."

RESPONSIBILITY
AND REBELLION
Genesis 2:4b–3:24

A new episode clearly begins with the introduction "In the day that the LORD God made the earth and the heavens" (2:4b). Having read in Gen. 1 a full account of the creation of the world and everything in it, we now find ourselves at a time when plants, animals, and people have not yet been created. This second major division of Genesis begins in a way that had become traditional for creation stories of various kinds in the ancient Near East. Many of them are introduced with an expression like "when there was not yet . . . ," followed by a list, longer or shorter, of things that did not exist when the story begins. This is exactly what we find in 2:4b-5: "When Yahweh God made the earth and the heavens, there was not yet any shrub of the field on the earth nor had any plant of the field yet sprouted. . . ." (author's translation). This forms a very appropriate beginning for a new unit, but we have noted that v. 4a also sounds like a suitable title, and it has been taken as such by many interpreters, ancient and modern. Certainly it now functions as a transitional clause between the full account of creation provided by P and a story about creation with very different intentions, which continues through chs. 2 and 3.

Earlier interpreters assumed 2:4b-25 was a "flashback," a retelling of the events of day six in more detail, but since the 19th cent. critical scholarship has agreed that this is a completely different version of creation. The full evidence for this conclusion must be sought elsewhere, but briefly we may note the difference in order of creation (man first, then the trees of Eden, the animals, and finally woman), the way the action of God is described ("And God said, 'Let there be . . . ,'" "and God made," "and God created" in ch. 1, contrasted with forming a figure out of dust and later performing surgery on him, in ch. 2), and the change from Elohim ("God") to Yahweh Elohim (rendered "LORD God" in most translations, although Yahweh is a proper name and does not mean "LORD"). As noted in the Introduction, the source critical approach to Genesis has assigned this section to the "Yahwistic source" (J), so called because the divine

33

name, Yahweh, is used from the very beginning; by contrast, the Priestly (P) and Elohistic (E) sources use the common Hebrew word for God, Elohim, throughout Genesis and do not introduce the name Yahweh until Exod. 6:2 and 3:15, respectively. For the past century of scholarship the Yahwist has usually been dated in the 10th cent. B.C., in the time of Solomon or shortly after, and he is thought to have been Judean, closely associated with Jerusalem in the early years of the Monarchy. Recently this early dating has been challenged and J has been connected instead with the end of the Monarchy, but these hypothetical dates will not greatly influence the interpretation offered here. Studies that have found very close relationships between the J materials in Genesis and the careers of David and Solomon will be profoundly affected by the question of date, but I have not found the association with those kings to be that obvious. The Mesopotamian epics of Gilgamesh and Adapa, in which we find partial parallels to the materials in Genesis, carry a heavy emphasis on kingship, and by comparison these chapters of Genesis seem to represent mostly different concerns.

Scholars continue to challenge the division of Gen. 1–11 into two sources, J and P, but none has succeeded as yet in offering a more satisfactory explanation of the differences between chs. 1 and 2. Evidence has been produced to show the unity of chs. 1–11, but this is best ascribed to the work of the redactor who carefully combined the sources. The interpretations offered here are based to a great extent on the acceptance of radical differences between the two chapters and on the explanation which postulates different authors and different audiences with different needs, living at different times.

Some interpreters also question whether chs. 2–3 form a continuous story produced by the same author, and others claim that some if not all the material assigned to J should be dated much later than the 10th cent. But we can find considerable evidence for the unity of chs. 2 and 3, and the interpretation of the story that will be offered here is based on its present form.

The Yahwist's Special Use of Creation Materials

Although 2:4b-6 take us back to (or near to) the beginning of the world, J has not attempted to provide a comprehensive account of how the world came into existence, as P did. He is concerned with the damage done to a series of relationships that are crucial to human life: between people and God, people and the material world, man and woman. In order to introduce these subjects, he uses some of the traditions about creation which were known in his time. As a result, much that is of great interest to P (such as the sea and the heavenly bodies) is completely ignored; we are left with very incomplete information about other things as well, since they were of no great interest to the author. Understanding that his purpose is not to present a complete creation story will free us from struggling with some of the unanswerable questions that have puzzled past interpreters.

The Creation story of Gen. 1:1–2:4a intends to describe the world we live in—admittedly in a very optimistic way—but the creation materials in Gen. 2–3 are very different. They speak of situations about which human beings know nothing from personal experience. No one has ever lived in Eden, or lived in complete isolation from all other living creatures, or known a life with no tensions between man and woman. No one has been confronted by a tree of life, a tree of the knowledge of good and evil, or a talking serpent. But these elements, representing a world none of us has ever known, make it possible for J to tell a story that depicts the predicament in which we all are involved. They can only be misunderstood if his story is thought to be a historical account of what happened to two people who lived long ago in a world utterly different from ours. The contortions that earlier interpreters performed in seeking to understand these chapters as the history of one man and one woman, Adam and Eve, can be eliminated once we understand what this story is really about.

The Genre—Saga, or Archetypal Story

What kind of literature did J produce in Gen. 2–3? It is certainly different from P's Creation account, which contained no tension, no plot, and could scarcely be called a story. Eventually, J develops a true masterpiece of storytelling, in ch. 3; but ch. 2 is not quite a full-fledged story. It is an extended preface, establishing the conditions that produce the tensions of ch. 3 and enable us to recognize ourselves in it. Now, a story (i.e., a narrative with a plot, a beginning, middle, and end) may be a fragment of "history," with characters and events that can be dated and located in known places; or it may be a free creation of the mind. All too often, interpreters of Scripture have assumed that only the former can be "true," ignoring the rather obvious use of "fictitious" stories in order to convey truth (see, e.g., the parables of Jesus). Form critical studies of the stories in Genesis have found evidence that they lie somewhere between a purely imaginative story (such as the parable) and straightforward accounts of historical events. Most of the materials in Gen. 12–50 probably have their roots in historical characters and events, but in their present form they are not told as "history," as something that happened once for all in the past. Rather, they represent the retelling and reapplication of events that tend to reoccur, generation after generation. So they take on their fullest meaning not as accounts of what happened to some long-dead ancestors, such as Abraham and Sarah or Adam and Eve. They make their fullest impact on us when we recognize that the experiences of Abraham and Sarah were recapitulated again and again in the life of Israel, and that Israel told these stories as self-affirmations, exercises in self-understanding. We may also discover ourselves in at least some of them. When that happens we will realize that those who insist on finding proof that exactly those events happened to certain characters in the past (attempting to equate "truth" with "historicity") may be insulating us from hearing them as a word from God directly to us.

An adequate term to designate this type of literature has yet to be found in English. "Saga" and "legend" are misleading, and "tale" is vague. I am tempted to call them "archetypal stories," as an effort to show how they functioned for Israel and can function for us; but I am by no means satisfied with that designation. The term "archetype" is of some value to us, however, as we consider how and why J selected some creation traditions and developed them into the story of the disobedience of Eve and Adam. As long as we think of Gen. 2–3 as a story about what happened to "those people," we miss its point. Once we recognize their experiences as archetypal, repeated in each of us, then we recognize them as *our* stories and it becomes increasingly hard to escape the word they direct immediately to us.

So, by beginning with life in the garden of Eden, which none of us has ever experienced, J is able to express his judgment of real life, with its endless toil in the effort to prolong a precarious existence (3:17b-19). The story of how the animals and the woman were created enables him to comment on our close, but uncertain—if not hostile—relationships with the animal kingdom and between men and women. And the mysterious trees with the forbidden fruit, which none of us has ever encountered, provides for him a vivid way by which he can entice us to relive our own experiences of disobedience and destructive self-assertion. In each case the difference between "then and now" in his narrative does not represent any meaningful chronological change, for such chronological changes (from Paradise to reality) do not occur in ordinary human life. Rather, the difference between then and now represents his judgment of the real world, the conclusion that something is radically wrong with this world. It is his way of asserting that the main fault for this condition lies in the rebellious behavior of human beings toward the God who made them and wants them to live in a good world, but who insists upon certain limits they must respect. It is that problem of limits and our refusal to accept them which dominates the outlook of J and makes his treatment of creation materials so different from P. If, as has been suggested, the Yahwistic account was produced in a time when Israel had power (Solomon's reign), we can easily understand why this might have been his major concern and why it would be so different from P's message to an exiled people. But it is more important for us to recognize J's narrative as the story of every individual, family, or institution with power enough to be tempted to determine its own destiny, without regard to the God to whom we all are responsible.

Unnecessary Questions

If it is correct to read this as our story, then its meaning is to be found in the plot, in the way the action develops, in the course of the narrative itself, and not in who the characters were, when and where they lived, or in any of the incidental details that are necessary for it to be a story and not a lecture about disobedience. This means that a great many of the questions over which casual readers and great interpreters alike have struggled really do not need to be answered, for they are irrelevant to what the story wants to say to us. That is because what happens in this story is what always happens, regardless of characters or circumstances, when there is temptation, disobedience, guilt, and punishment.

If this is the correct approach—and I am convinced it is—then here are some examples of unnecessary, useless questions. Others will be noted in the course of the interpretation.

Did Adam and Eve eat of the fruit of the tree of life before they were expelled from the garden? If they had not sinned, would they have lived forever?
This is irrelevant, because it corresponds to nothing in any human life we know anything about. We know of no one who lives forever or who has barely missed the chance to do so.

Were they conscious of their sexuality before eating the fruit? Were they sexually active?
We do not need instruction about human beings who are not conscious of sex.

What was this "knowledge of good and evil" that they did not have before eating the fruit and that they did have afterwards?

That might seem to be the key to the story, but in fact it is not an essential question. Whatever it is, we all have it now (3:22), and the change of condition when "their eyes were opened" is not a change that has occurred to anyone we know.

What exactly was "the human" (ha'adam) *in ch. 2 before God made the woman from his side: an ordinary male, an androgynous being, or what?*

It is a waste of time to try to answer such a question, for we know human beings only as male and female and have no experience of any other kind of *adam* ("human"). The question should be why the author found it appropriate to describe the creation of humanity as a two-stage process, for in that we shall find his comments on life as we live it now.

The story is so fascinating that our imaginations inevitably grab it and want to run with it, to fill in the details, explain the omissions, expand on the motivations. That is one way of making it our own story. The answers that interpreters have offered to questions such as those I have dismissed above reveal a great deal of what they believe about God and think about themselves. But if we are to allow the account to remain *J's* word to us (which I believe to be *God's* word to us), without forcing it to become the story *we* want it to be, then restraint is called for. Let us assume that J tells us what he wants us to know, that what he emphasizes is important, and that what he skims over lightly, fails to explain, or leaves out was unimportant to him and thus we should not dwell on it. It is doubtful that we can improve on J's story by inventing answers for the questions he left unanswered, so let us try to resist that temptation.

GOD CREATES "THE HUMAN" AND GIVES HIM A PLACE TO LIVE (2:4b-17)

Creation of "the Human" (2:4b-7)

This passage begins with a long, complicated sentence, vv. 4b-7, which contains a good many elements that will not be of any importance in the development of the story. Its purpose is little more than to tell us that this is a story about the beginnings of things. J uses the traditional "when there was not yet . . ." introduction that appears in many ancient Near Eastern creation stories, and he focuses on fertility: no shrubs or plants, no rain, no man to till the soil. It is only the last of these elements that really interests him, for the creation of shrubs and plants is never mentioned, nor does he say anything more about rain. The subject of the story, *ha'adam* ("the human"), has appeared, however, and in an appropriate context, in connection with working the ground so that plants may grow for food. That is his role both at the beginning and the end of the story, but the nature of the work will change drastically. The intimate relationship between the human and the ground is emphasized by the play on words in Hebrew between *adam* ("human") and *adamah* ("ground, earth"). Some have tried to reproduce the similarity of words by translating *adam* as "earthling" or "earth creature." I have not yet seen "human" and "humus" suggested as an alternative. At any rate, *adam* has the definite article *(ha)* attached, so it is not the name Adam. We once would say "the Man" or "Mankind," but those terms are no longer acceptable. "The human being" is probably best, but becomes clumsy, so I have chosen to treat the adjective "human" as a noun (as it has been used in English since the 16th cent. and so is no novelty) and to use it with apologies for its rather unpleasant sound.

Before telling about the creation of the human, J includes a rather mystifying insertion about the *ed*, which "went up from the earth and watered the whole face of the ground" (v. 6). The RSV translates it "mist," but the word also appears in Akkadian, where it refers to an underground stream. Its place here is puzzling. We have been told there were no shrubs or plants because there was no rain, but now learn of a kind of fountain that waters the whole earth. Nothing more is said of it. Is the fountain the source of the river that flows out of Eden (v. 10)? We are not told. This seems to reflect a contradiction, perhaps the result of combining the creation traditions of two different areas, a place like Palestine, where rain is essential, and one like Mesopotamia, where irrigation provided the necessary water. If v. 6 originated in Mesopotamia, J might have kept it because it provided a third word play; in the consonantal Hebrew text appear, within six words, *'dm* ("human"), *'dmh* ("ground"), and *'d* ("stream"). At any rate, it plays no further role in the story.

Having described in a long subordinate clause (vv. 4b-6) the conditions at the time the human was made, J now comes in v. 7 to the first divine act of interest to him, and this is told in detail. The human is "formed" or "shaped" of dust from the ground, using a verb that can be used of the work of a potter (2 Sam. 17:28; Isa. 29:16; Jer. 18:2, 3, 4), but is most often used to describe the creative work of God. It is likely that the common idea, repeated here, that humans were made from dust came from observation of the end of human existence, that the body does eventually become a part of the soil. The way in which God is said to have given life to the body, breathing into his nostrils the breath of life, was probably also based on observation, for the absence of breath is one of the most obvious indications of death. What we know about—the way human existence ends—has been projected back to provide a vivid picture of something we have not experienced: the creation of a human being. Note that Ezekiel's vision of the restoration of life to the dead follows the same pattern (Ezek. 37:1-10).

Body plus breath produces a *nephesh hayyah* (RSV "living being"; KJV "living soul"). The word *hayyah* means "life"; *nephesh* has a range of meanings, from "throat," "breath," to "person"; but it is never used in Hebrew to denote some spiritual part of a person that can exist without the body, so it does not correspond to the Greek idea of the soul. The "living *nephesh*" is the result of the combination of body and breath (when the OT speaks of a "dead *nephesh*" it specifically means a corpse; Lev. 21:11; Num. 6:6). The same expression, *nephesh hayyah,* is used of the animals in Gen. 2:19, although the RSV and KJV conceal this somewhat by translating it "living creature." The Israelite view of human existence was thus a wholistic one: life consists in having an animated body. Since the Israelites did not conceive of life without a body, this eventually resulted in the Jewish belief in life after death as a resurrection of the body, rather than the life of an immortal soul in heaven.

A Place to Live: The Garden (2:8-15)

Unlike P, J provides a reason why God created human beings. According to v. 5 it was to have someone to work the ground, which sounds much like the reasons given in Mesopotamian creation stories, where people are usually said to have been made to do the gods' work for them. This next section of the story moves away from that kind of explanation, however, for after making the human, God takes care to provide a good place in which he may live. As in Gen. 1, the earth is made for the benefit of human beings, although J describes it in a quite different way. He focuses on one special place made by God for human life, a garden. In the Middle East the garden represented nature in its ideal form. It would typically have a wall around it to protect it from the incursions of animals and would be well-watered and cultivated—a pleasant, secure, and fertile place (cf. Isa. 5:1-6; 27:2-5). God thus provides nature "under control" for the human, filled with fruit trees, a place of both beauty and usefulness (Gen. 2:9). Its location, in Eden, is probably another of J's plays on words, for the same word means "delight" or "pleasure" in 2 Sam. 1:24; Ps. 36:8. Whether J knew of the actual place in Mesopotamia named Eden (2 Kgs. 19:12; Ezek. 27:23) we do not know, but that probably would not have been of great interest to him. He simply locates it vaguely somewhere in the east, and all efforts to improve on his geography have failed. We will not engage here in the futile effort to map the four rivers and their regions (Gen. 2:11-14), for the place names given do not correspond to the geography of any period that we know. As Karl Barth commented, Eden was a real place on earth, yet one which cannot be investigated. The description of the river and its branches is important because it affirms Eden to be the center of the world and the source of life for the rest of it. Eden does not exist for us, nor did it exist for Israel; but what they said about Eden, locating it in the real world as they did, was Israel's statement about the world in which we all do live. Here is the bold affirmation that this world is a place not totally unlike Eden, so that in it we can find a home. It is a corrupted and polluted garden in which we live, that is true; but there are enough similarities to Eden that we can know what this world ought to be like. From the Bible's description of Eden we can know what God intends life in this world to be like and can see some clues pointing toward what we may do about some of its present corruption.

For the human is not just put in the garden to live and do nothing. He is given work to do (v. 15): he is to till it and keep it. The word translated "till" means "to work," "to serve." From this root come words meaning "servant," "work," and "worship." In this case, the human is not to serve the ground, but to work it, and that is part of his blessing. The word translated "keep" often means "to watch over" or "guard"; we may wonder about its appropriateness here, for what dangers might threaten Eden at this point? The word fits the description of the Middle Eastern garden, however, with its emphasis on security, and we may say that at this point the human is not so much to guard it as to be responsible for it.

In the middle of that garden are two unique trees, the tree of life and the tree of the knowledge of good and evil (v. 9). Since the former does not become a factor in the story until the very end (3:22), it seems most appropriate to reserve discussion of it for that point; otherwise we should need to presuppose much that comes later. The tree of knowledge, however, becomes the focal point of the story. "Good and evil" have been taken in their moral sense, simply awareness of the difference between good and bad; in their practical sense, the experience of the effects of the two courses of action; and in a much more narrow sense, as the knowledge of acceptable and unacceptable sexual behavior. The most common explanation takes the two words as extremes bracketing all of life, so that knowledge of good and evil would mean virtual omniscience. One interesting suggestion links good and evil with another pair, life and death, since only humans know that they will die. And the discussion continues. The author either assumes his readers know exactly what the concept means, so does not bother to explain it, or does not think one needs to know about "good and evil" in order to understand his story. What have the man and woman acquired after they eat that forbidden fruit? Shame (compare 2:25 and 3:7) and fear (3:10). Should we imagine that J equated these emotions with knowledge of good and evil? Is it not rather true that the shame and fear came not from the tree but from the act of eating, i.e., from the act of disobedience? I believe it is not necessary to solve the riddle of what "knowledge of good and evil" may have meant to J, for he does not seem to care greatly about it. The key to his story is not how the attributes of primal humanity changed because of the ingestion of some "magic fruit," but is the question of whether it is possible to obey God. Everyone J knew and everyone we know has the knowledge of good and evil, according to his story; no one exists in the primal state of Gen. 2. But the question of obedience is still as alive as ever, and it is disobedience that produces shame and fear. If we focus on what gifts that tree of knowledge might have given two ancestors of the human race, we deal with irrelevancies; but if we put ourselves in their place, facing something desirable but forbidden, needing to decide whether to obey or not, then we see that this story is real life, and that its concern is the human act of decision, and nothing supernatural or primordial.

We have completed the setting for the story proper: the ground has been made fertile; neither desert nor jungle are concerns, for there is a garden in which to live; and there is a human being to work it, to keep it, and to enjoy it. Now the first step toward the real world can be taken, in 2:16, with the setting of limits, raising the question of obedience, initiating the tension that will lead eventually to failure.

Limits: The Forbidden Tree (Gen. 2:16-17)

God's goodness and his intention to bless the human had been suggested by his provision of the garden; now that is emphasized by his first word to his new creation, making every tree in the garden available to him—except one. But why, we may ask, should there have been any exceptions, if the garden was made for the human? Why not everything? And surely that is exactly the reaction to this restriction that would be expected, if it is really our story.

Here is one of the places where the kind of God one believes in is very likely to have a strong influence on how one understands the story. Some cannot help but see the knowledge of good and evil as something that God arbitrarily and unworthily decides to withhold. Others question whether it was a test that God knew in advance the human would fail. In either case, the story is read so as to make the human the helpless victim of a cruel God. But the issue, once again, is not the content conveyed by the fruit—knowledge of good and evil—but the nature of the relationship between human beings and God; and the way we read the story itself, thus putting ourselves into it, reflects the kind of relationship we have with our God.

So far the human has been absolutely dependent on God, for life and everything he has. The question now is, will he accept that relationship and be content with it? There is a prior question, however: Does he have any choice? The setting of a limit shows that he does indeed have a choice and thus establishes his freedom. If there had been no limits he would have had no choices to make, and could not have been called a free person. But God allows him to decide for or against the relationship that he has established with him.

What more does the human need at this point in order to enjoy the good life? He needs something more, the story tells us later, but it is not the knowledge of good and evil. It is a partner, and God continues to show his loving care by providing the partner. So J never suggests that the choice to eat the forbidden fruit might give the human something that is important to have. All that is asked here is to affirm what God affirms and to deny what God denies; that is all that is asked of us. Yet this seems an oppressive limit, as we recognize when we see that ch. 3 is *our* story. As Paul Ricoeur put it, ". . . We no longer know what a limit that does not repress, but orients and guards freedom, could be like . . . . We are acquainted only with the limit that constrains" (*The Symbolism of Evil*, 250). So it is hard to accept the truth that it is by setting limits for us that God establishes our freedom.

"You shall not eat" (2:17). Eating is one of the key themes in these chapters. The word is used sixteen times, and here it forms the only prohibition that God places before the human. Why should God's only law at the beginning involve eating—a mere peccadillo, as one interpreter called it, compared with real sins such as the murder in ch. 4? So far it has been emphasized that it is not the nature of the

sin but the relationship that it destroys which is crucial to our understanding of the story; but some further consideration of eating may
be enlightening. Is not eating the most essential physical activity for
the preservation of life? In Gen. 1 the only specific provision God
made for the living beings he created was what they might eat. In
this chapter, God makes two provisions, for food and for compan-
ionship. But the symbolic significance of eating has been a powerful
one in Judaism and Christianity. The first great festival to be pro-
claimed was Passover, celebrated by means of a meal. One of the earliest prohibitions in Scripture involves the eating of blood (Gen.
9:4). Israel was to show its continued faithfulness to God by carefully observing regulations about what could be eaten and how it
could be prepared. In Christianity, the one sacrament that is observed by believers again and again is the Lord's Supper, but all other
eating has been desacralized. Hence it may be seen that the prohibition of Gen. 2:17 is not completely trivial; if the great sin of ch. 4
has to do with death, this one is concerned with life.

The penalty for eating the forbidden fruit, however, is death, "for
in the day that you eat of it you shall die." This RSV translation is
inaccurate. "In the day" is too literal, for the Hebrew expression does
not denote one twenty-four hour period, but is the ordinary way to
say "when." And the force of the penalty has been lost, for it should
say, "you shall surely die." Yet Adam ate the fruit and lived on for
930 years! Was the serpent telling the literal truth when he said, "You
will not surely die" (3:4 author's translation)? Many interpreters
here allude to what we can learn from the OT about the Hebrew understanding of death as a condition that may begin before one lies
down never to rise again. Death often is connected directly with
being cut off from God (Job 7:21; Ps. 88:5, 10-12; Isa. 38:18-19),
and that is what begins to happen at the end of Gen. 3. John Calvin
said the miseries in which Adam involved himself by his disobedience were a kind of entrance into death, until death itself entirely
absorbed him. This corresponds with what modern studies have revealed about the OT concept (cf. Ezekiel's use of "live" and "die" in
Ezek. 18, where the terms have nothing to do with the infliction of
the death penalty).

Karl Barth claimed that "You shall surely die" was not a threat or
a punishment, but a protective measure, a warning against the effects
of eating. If so, then it seems J has also permitted a discordant element into his account of God's good creation, before the occurrence
of human sin, somewhat comparable to the threat of Gen. 1:2 that
led to the commission given to human beings to subdue the earth in

v. 28. Here we have learned of a good God who placed into a beautiful and useful garden a human made from the earth, with no faults worth mentioning. But in that garden is not only the tree of life, which surely represents God's intention for the future of humanity, but another tree, which is both a possibility and a threat. It is possible for the human to obey, hence maintaining the good relationship God established, but it is also possible for him to rebel. How could that be? J could not explain it any more than we or any of the greatest theologians and philosophers of Judaism and Christianity. But J knew the tree must be there, for it represents life as we know it. We are faced by decisions; we do encounter the temptations to be our own gods, or gods to other people; and in one way or another, that choice leads to death.

GOD MAKES THE HUMAN COMPLETE (2:18-25)

The Animal World: No Fit Companions for the Human (2:18-20)

God now makes a most surprising statement. There is something in his created work that is not good (2:18). As we have seen, P would never have included such a statement, for he emphasized the goodness of all that God made at every step of the way. What can J have in mind? Does he speak of a sort of trial and error procedure, as some commentators have suggested; or could it be that he is more clever than that and is introducing into his narrative a tension that does not reflect on God's wisdom, but is instead an accurate reflection of some of the tensions of human existence? Let us try out the latter reading.

The expression "not good" usually denotes something that is morally reprehensible, but that is obviously not its meaning here. Sometimes it means untrustworthy (1 Sam. 29:6), unwise (2 Sam. 17:7), unhealthful (Prov. 25:27), or simply not conducive to one's well-being (Prov. 19:2). The last must be its meaning here. God is not necessarily speaking of something evil (the usual opposite to good) about his work but of an acknowledged inadequacy, which he intends to correct immediately. So we move to J's two-stage process of the creation of humanity with the question in mind all along, as to why it should have been told that way.

The conclusion of Gen. 2:18 is crucial: "I will make him a helper fit for him." The history of interpretation of these words is a strange one. The KJV reads "an help meet for him," an accurate translation, understanding "meet" to mean, in 17th-cent. English, "appropriate." Some of us may still read, in the communion service, "it is meet and right so to do." But somehow the two words became combined into "helpmeet," then altered to "helpmate," a distortion of the Hebrew and of what KJV meant. Furthermore, the cultural subordination of woman led virtually every interpreter to understand the "helping" here in terms of the domestic duties thought to be appropriate for woman, thinking of helpers as those who work for someone else. Those who believe the story is really speaking of an intended equality of men and women have then focused on the word translated "meet" or "fit" as well as other elements in the passage. But fifteen of the twenty-one occurrences of *'ezer* ("help") in the OT refer to God, and the others (except for Gen. 2:18, 20) indicate the inadequacy of human help. So the helper normally designated by this word is one with superior power, not a subordinate in any sense. "Our help is in the name of the LORD, who made heaven and earth" (e.g., Ps. 124:8; cf. 115:9-11; 121:1-2; Deut. 33:7, 26, 29). But in this story, God does not intend to be the human's helper; he needs another kind, one "fit" for him or, better, "corresponding to" him, of his own kind. For it is not good to be alone. Loneliness is frequently spoken of in the OT as a situation involving more than the unhappiness, the emotional distress so familiar to us. It may also involve danger (e.g., Lev. 13:46; Isa. 27:10; Jer. 15:17; Lam. 1:1; 3:28). When this is added to the knowledge that the help that God usually gives in these texts is deliverance from danger, the seriousness of the problem described in Gen. 2:18 becomes more clear. Recently it has been suggested that "partner" or "companion" would be superior translations of *'ezer,* for they would appropriately suggest the equality of the woman; but in fact they are not strong enough. What is needed is someone to deliver the human from his solitude, the kind of thing that ordinarily God does; but God determines that a solitary relationship between the human and his maker is not adequate. If he is to be complete, he must have a helper who is like him, his equivalent.

So God makes a lot of animals. Surely God knew better than that! Of course he did, but this is a story, and by telling it this way J shows us our proper relationship to the animal world. The relationship is very close; the animals were formed out of the ground, as humans were, and both are called *nephesh hayyah,* "living beings." The KJV and RSV are deceptive here, since both translate the term in 2:19 "living creature," but the same term in v. 7 is rendered "living being" in the RSV and "living soul" in KJV. The NEB is helpful by reading "living creature" in both places. Another aspect of the relationship appears in the naming process. In Hebrew thought that means the human understood them—knew what they were—and he assumed power over them. To give a name was a statement about what that someone really was (cf. Gen. 4:1, 25; 1 Sam. 1:20), and changing a name was a sign of power (cf. Dan. 1:7). But, pet lovers to the contrary, the animals cannot fill the need described in Gen. 2:18. The OT would not agree with the saying, "The more I see of people, the better I like my dog." For the human can assume mastery over the animals, and the relationship is an easy one, in that respect. But something more complex, more intimate, a full two-way relationship is needed, despite the difficulties that causes. So God makes the woman.

Man and Woman (2:21-23)

We cannot visualize what happens now. What sort of creature had "the human" (*ha'adam*) been, that part of him could be built up into a woman and what was left over was then a man? Even to formulate such a question is so difficult that we ought to be warned against trying to make too much of this scene. The author's very choice of vocabulary thwarts every effort at a description of such an event.

The human who had participated in the creation of the animals is now put into a "deep sleep" by God. We think immediately of anesthesia and of a major job of plastic surgery, but the Hebrews had no knowledge of such things. They used this word (*tardemah*) to denote an unnaturally deep state of unconsciousness, usually one induced by God himself (e.g., Gen. 15:12; Job 33:15; Isa. 29:10; cf. Ps. 76:5; Dan. 8:18; 10:9; natural causes: Prov. 19:15; cf. 10:5; Judg. 4:21; Jonah 1:5). Not only is it impossible for the human to produce another like himself; he cannot experience what is happening nor know how it is done. For what is told here is not archetypal, not something experienced again and again so that we recognize ourselves in it; it is completely different from anything we know or can imagine. We know ourselves only as men and women. The function of this strange incident is to lay before us the inevitability of what we do know: the mystery of our unity as human beings despite the puzzling differences resulting from our sexuality.

The mystery is deepened by the use of the word *tsela'* to denote the part that God took from the human. Despite the traditional translation "rib," we do not know to what part of the body that refers. This is the only place the word is used of part of a human body; elsewhere it always refers to something connected with the side of a sacred structure, the ark of the covenant, the tabernacle, the altars, or the temple (except 2 Sam. 16:13, where it is a hillside). The verb denoting what God did with this part of the human's side is an appropriate accompaniment of a term usually connected with structures, for it is the common word meaning "build"; but nowhere else is it used of God's creative work. Odd speculations can be found in the older literature about why that verb is used of the formation of woman, but it is wise to take seriously Claus Westermann's comment that this "should not be understood as a description of an actual event accessible to us."

Sexist interpretations in the past have made much of the masculine gender of *ha'adam,* saying "man" was created first, then woman. This leaves us open to a choice between two sexist readings: either that man is primary and woman a kind of afterthought, or that man was the first, imperfect experiment and woman the culmination of the whole process. Both should be rejected, for J shows no indication of interest in the question of primacy or superiority; indeed, the whole emphasis of the passage is on equality. That is an important message to us, and it is remarkable that in the patriarchal culture of ancient Israel such a message was heard and allowed to stand as a part of the sacred writings, even though it may not have been acted on with much effectiveness. Indeed, this is the only creation story known from the ancient Near East that gives to woman such an important role. It has stood for centuries, often—but not always—unheeded, as a radical challenge to the assumption of male supremacy. Jesus clearly heard it and acted upon it, and in our day we may rejoice in new efforts to understand its implications for life in family, Church, and society.

The masculine gender of *adam* may have been of some theological value, despite the ways it has been misused. If some noun in the feminine gender had been used to represent humanity, would not a story such as this have inevitably been misinterpreted as the archetype of giving birth? Then a naturalistic explanation of the existence of the human race would have been possible. But men do not give birth and so can take no credit whatever for the event of Gen. 2:21-23, which remains a mystery, the work of God alone. Man and woman are the gift of God to one another.

"And he brought her to the man." Now comes the great recognition scene. The man has been in a coma, but he knows what this is, for he recognizes part of himself in her. Modern translations appropriately recognize his words to be poetry—the Bible's first poetry. The man's first quoted words are a love song. It has often been claimed that the perfect equality between man and woman, emphasized in the first part of this section and reemphasized in "bone of my bones and flesh of my flesh," is compromised when he gives her a name, "woman," thus presumably claiming primacy over her; but that is a misreading. It was God who made this new being a woman (v. 22), and the man's words are a recognition of her relationship to him, not an act of naming as found in 1:5; 2:19-20. He makes a play on the Hebrew words *ishshah* ("woman") and *ish* ("man") as another way of acknowledging the intimacy of their relationship. This is the first time these standard words for man and woman have been used in the story, and *adam* takes on an ambiguity from this point on. "The woman" *(ishshah)* is referred to regularly from 2:22 through 4:1 and sometimes "the man" *(ish)* is used (2:23, 24; 3:6, 16); but "the human" *(ha'adam)* continues to be used, now representing the male partner in this marriage rather than humanity as a whole. Eventually we shall give up and use the word as a proper name, Adam, but translators have never been able to agree where it is proper to begin doing that (see comment on 3:20).

Marriage (2:24-25)

The deficiency in the human's condition—indeed his distress, if the force in Hebrew of the words "alone" and "helper" is emphasized—has been alleviated, and humanity is now complete, in the form of man and woman. They belong together, and so J very naturally moves to a comment on the institution of marriage. This is one of the most obvious indicators of J's awareness that he is writing our story and not just the history of two unique, primordial individuals, for 2:24 does not apply to them at all: they had no parents. J is not even interested in the customs of his own patriarchal culture, in which the woman left her household to join the man, but is speaking of something more fundamental about the relationship of man and woman. It is so powerful that it transcends the ties of blood, the lifelong emotional bonds that hold child to parent. The woman in his day might have no choice but to leave her home, because her father arranged a marriage for her; so it is the man, who had more freedom, of whom J speaks. He finds his full identity not in his associations with parents and siblings, but in free and full commitment to a woman.

Unfortunately there is little of comfort here for the homosexual or for those who never marry, for whatever reason. The Israelites did not find any blessings in the single state (cf. Jer. 16:1-4). In the NT Paul has begun to think of some valid reasons for remaining single. But lest those who are married consider themselves superior to the single, or the single conclude that the OT simply omits them from serious attention, it should be noted that J will soon remind us that marriage is far from perfect and that those who are married experience both joys and a depth of pain that the single may never know.

Nowhere else does the OT speak of "becoming one flesh," but expressions such as "you are my bone and my flesh" (Gen. 29:14) are used to indicate the closest kind of interpersonal relationships (cf. 37:27; Judg. 9:2-3; 2 Sam. 5:1; 19:13). The phrase does not have any specific sexual connotations, but insists that the married couple becomes a new unit, socially and emotionally. We can scarcely imagine the Israelites not assuming that the physical unity of intercourse was included, if they took this to be their own story.

"And the two of them were naked, the man *(ha'adam)* and his wife, and they were not ashamed of themselves (or, 'of one another')" (author's translation). The verb is the common Hebrew word for shame, but nowhere else is it used in this form, which can be either reflexive or reciprocal in meaning. Nakedness elsewhere in the OT often indicates a defenseless or miserable condition, but that scarcely seems to fit this context. It is directly associated with sexual intercourse in Lev. 18 (23 times); 20:18, 19; 1 Sam. 20:30; Ezek. 16:36; 23:18, so its implication here may well be that the ideal relationship between husband and wife—including intercourse—involves no barriers of any kind, no self-consciousness, but complete and unhindered giving and enjoying of one another.

Nakedness is also associated with the word for "shame" in 1 Sam. 20:30; Isa. 20:2-5; Mic. 1:11 (cf. Hos. 2:5, 9; Ezek. 16) and describes situations the Israelites clearly considered shameful in Gen. 9:22-23; Lev. 20:18-19; Isa. 3:17; 47:3; Lam. 1:8 and elsewhere. Only in Gen. 2:25 is a naked person explicitly said not to be ashamed, and what follows in 3:7-11 makes it clear that the man and woman are not being condemned for their lack of shame. This verse is one of the keys to the pathos of chs. 2–3. It speaks of a condition that does not exist in our world, of people without awareness of themselves as autonomous units over against other selves, but living in communion with another without the need for defenses—and clothes are our first line of defense. Gen. 2:25 expresses J's judgment that God did not intend us to live with barriers isolating one from another, that such a need indicates something has gone radically wrong with our relationships with other human beings—and with our God (3:10). The appearance of nakedness as an issue in ch. 3, after the self-assertion of the woman and the man, shows us that 2:25 is far more important than a statement about the idyllic sexual relationship that is possible between man and woman; it uses the elementary concepts of nakedness and shame to lay bare the dilemma of us all—that because we think of ourselves as "I"—in distinction from, over against, and in competition with others (God included)—then we need defenses, and walls are built, and shame and fear are our lot.

THE DECLARATION OF INDEPENDENCE (3:1-13)

Opportunity (3:1-6)

All of ch. 2 sets the stage for the story of ch. 3, which begins immediately with the Bible's first conversation. We have been well prepared for most of the developments in this chapter: relationships between man and woman and between God and humans have been clearly delineated, God's care to provide a good place to live in the garden has been emphasized, and the limits defining human freedom have been established by the tree from which they have been forbidden to eat. But we are not prepared for the first development, the introduction of a fourth character, the serpent. No specific reference to any one animal had been made in 2:19-20, and it is introduced here with the utmost brevity, as "more subtle than any other wild creature that the LORD God had made" (3:1). Once again, J takes the play on words very seriously, for the similarity in sound between the word meaning "naked" *('arummim)* in 2:25 and the one meaning "subtle" *('arum)* in 3:1 seems to provide for him a satisfactory connective element between the two verses.

Why this fourth character, and why is it a serpent? Eventually, when the concept of a personal tempter, the source of evil—the devil—had developed, interpreters found it easy to identify the serpent with the devil or to say the devil worked through an actual snake. But this happened long after the OT period (cf. Wis. 2:24; Rev. 12:9; 20:2). Specific references to the satan (a Hebrew word meaning "adversary") occur in only three places in the OT: Job 1–2, where he is in the employ of God; Zech. 3:1-2, where he is the unrighteous accuser of the high priest; and 1 Chr. 21:1, where he is a tempter. The OT ordinarily does not speak of some evil, personal force in opposition to God and to some extent independent from him, as later Judaism and Christianity did in their development of the concept of Satan as a fallen angel, the tempter who brought evil into the world. The curse on the serpent in this chapter (Gen. 3:14-15) clearly shows that J is thinking of a real snake. The snake can talk;

but let us not worry too much about whether or how that could be, for the conversation is necessary if the story is to be told at all, and it is a unique and unrepeated occurrence. As such it is the least important element of the story, for the rest of it is typical, repeated regularly in human experience. The appearance of this unexpected fourth character is necessary in order for J to represent the experience of temptation accurately and in keeping with his understanding of God and humanity. He would not attribute the existence of sin to the will of God; neither could he admit that human will is in itself evil, and thus the source of sin. Temptation is certainly largely an internal process, but it seems to originate from without. If its source cannot be attributed to God or to human nature, what could the author say? He clearly rejected the belief in evil deities or spirits, which his polytheistic neighbors would have offered as an easy explanation, for his God is the Creator of all that is, and he made it all to be good. So J chooses one of God's creatures to become the source of temptation, and the snake is the best candidate. It had an ambiguous reputation in the ancient East, sometimes represented as the source of wisdom or healing or immortality in other religions, but always presented negatively in the OT, as a strange creature to be feared. It is not called evil here, for it is one of the creatures God made. Rather, it is described as possessing one decidedly ambiguous quality, this "subtlety" (RSV) or "craftiness" (NEB) or "cunningness" (TEV). Forms of this word are used fifteen other places in the OT; ten of them (all in Proverbs) represent positive qualities, such as prudence, while the other five speak of negative attributes, such as cunning. It is evident that the author has selected and described his fourth character with great care.

As the conversation and its results in the woman's mind will show us, the serpent's "subtlety" is the ability to provoke reflection on the true meaning of freedom, to reveal by means of conversation that the woman had the ability to think for herself, to suggest to her that she had the power to decide for herself. So it is the course of the conversation that is truly important, and not the existence of a talking serpent. The snake is not necessarily an evil or a fallen being here, although the instinctive human hatred of snakes (reflected in the curse of vv. 14-15) made him a logical choice for the one who initiated the human grasp for independence. This creature is a tempter in a sense, but only as a catalyst, assisting the woman's own mental processes to discover the freedom she had the power to grasp. As other commentators have pointd out, the tempter tells the truth, but in a deceptive way.

The question why the tempter approached the woman rather than the man has been discussed for centuries, and almost inevitably the answers given have been sexist. The usual one is that the serpent began with the weaker party and through her was able to entice the man to sin (already found in 1 Tim. 2:14). But the opposite position has also been argued: the stronger person was approached first, knowing that if she could be convinced the battle was won. Both answers are sexist because the question itself is sexist. Both answers can be argued because J shows no interest in the question and makes no explicit comment on it. Apparently J is perfectly serious about the equality of the man and woman; one will serve just as well as the representative of humanity as would the other. Only the later insistence on Adam as primary and Eve as secondary led to the feeling that it was strange for Eve to take the primary role. As Gen. 3:20 shows, if Adam means "humanity," Eve means "life"; and so her experience in making the grasp for independence in vv. 1-6 is the experience of all of us. If men do not recognize themselves in this woman, then they allow the true force of this story to bypass them. Eve's reasoning process is not feminine; it is human.

The conversation begins with an indirectly worded question. Derek Kidner represents the effect of the Hebrew in this way: "So God has actually said. . . ." And then the serpent misrepresents God as one who is unkind and unfairly restrictive. This is the typical beginning of temptation: the suspicion of whether God really intends to be good to us, of whether God's way is really best, and the suggestion that one might be able to make one's own judgments about what is good, independent of anyone else.

But the woman knows better, and she is drawn by this misrepresentation to make a defense of God (vv. 2-3). Much has been made of the defects of her defense. It is obvious that she has added a prohibition not found in 2:17, "neither shall you touch it," and it may be that this suggests the beginnings of doubt in her mind. Others have found her paraphrase of the warning concerning death to be too weak ("lest you die" rather than "you shall surely die") and have thought she does not take the danger seriously enough. But suppose we give her (and ourselves in similar situations) the benefit of the doubt and consider it to be a perfectly innocent answer, so far. The real problem is that, by answering at all, the process of making her own judgments has begun. Conversation about God and his will has already involved some distortions, but the fatal flaw only comes when God falls into the background and the human will takes over.

The serpent takes the initiative now, in making an independent judgment, quoting the death penalty in his own, ambiguous way, so that we may translate it either, "You certainly will not die!" or "You will not certainly die." Is it a direct challenge, or just a suggestion that there might be a loophole somewhere? Sometimes it is the one that leads us on toward disobedience and sometimes the other. But next comes a promise, independent from and claiming to be superior to the promise of God, and once again casting doubt on God's goodwill toward the woman and man: "Your eyes will be opened, and you will be like God (or 'as gods')" (3:5). And this is the irresistible promise, the offer of independence. Here is represented in a simple and direct form that perennial human restlessness and dissatisfaction with whatever we may have—as long as we are aware of something more, which we do not yet possess. And the ultimate possession would be to be completely our own bosses, responsible to no one—to be like God.

That is an act of rebellion against our maker; and yet the subtlety, the apparently perfect reasonableness of much temptation, is skillfully represented in v. 6. The woman does not condemn God; we hear no direct questioning of God's good intentions, no outright denials or expressions of doubt. She just begins to think for herself. And what (we may respond) is so bad about that? Was it not God who gave her (us) the ability to reason, to make decisions? Unquestioning obedience in this world is so questionable that even when obedience to God is the subject, as it is here, we can scarcely accept it. In our experience we have found that in addition to the saints, with their unquestioning obedience, there are also the fanatics and mental cases. And those experiences make Eve's story inevitably our story, for they put us exactly where she is, facing a temptation that is convincingly reasonable and thus unavoidable.

She has learned that it is possible to think for herself, thus to take responsibility for her own life. But is she wise enough, is she good enough, does she have strength enough (substitute "we" for "she" in each case) to be independent? She soon learns the answer.

Consequences (3:7-13)

The serpent was partly right; the woman and the man eat the forbidden fruit but do not die immediately, and their eyes are opened. The story continues to be exactly accurate in its portrayal of reality as we know it, for what makes temptation so strong and sin so attractive is that it is indeed partly right. This tree—which was good for food, a delight to the eyes, and desired to make one wise—represents all those choices we make that seem to offer so much we want that we are willing to ignore the warnings attached, until our eyes are opened. What did they eat? It does not matter. Certainly it was not an apple; that idea is a contribution from writers in Latin, who could not resist a play on words of their own, between *malum,* meaning "evil," and *malum,* meaning "apple." The fruit is unimportant; what opened their eyes was not a magic substance but, rather, the act of eating. Deciding that it was good to eat, picking and eating taught them they had the freedom to disobey, to determine their own destinies.

Their eyes were opened, and the result was shame or, perhaps more accurately, self-consciousness. Having made their declaration of independence from God, they are now aware of themselves in a new way, as autonomous beings over against other selves. They know that they can exercise an independent will that differs from the wills of others, and they already sense (as we know so well from experience) that these differing wills are potentially hostile. The first act of their new state of knowledge is to attempt to create a defense. They are aware of themselves as naked, that is, as two different kinds of human beings and thus potentially enemies. Their pitiful garments of fig leaves, scratchy and sketchy, are their attempt to make clothing their first line of defense.

Moreover, when their eyes were opened they became afraid, and this was the beginning of death. Verses 8 and 10 display an ironic use of words. "They heard the sound (or 'voice') of the LORD God" uses three words that appear in God's commendation of Abraham in Gen. 22:18: "because you listened to my voice" (the RSV translates the verb "obeyed," but it is the same word that appears in 3:8). Ordinarily in Hebrew "listening" to God's voice means to "obey" him, but here the identical words lead to hiding, because they are afraid. Here is the second irony. The word for "fear" in Hebrew can mean terror, a reaction to danger; but it is also used to denote religious commitment, dedication to God, in the common expression "to fear the LORD." Adam's fear (v. 10) is the former, not the latter. Many have commented on the strong anthropomorphism of this verse, which speaks of the sound or voice of the LORD God walking about in the garden in the cool of the day, like any human garden-owner; but this may be seen as one of J's typically subtle ways of making a point. These few words make it possible for us to conceive of a divine-human community where God intends to be seen face-to-face; J tells us that such a community is God's intention, but it has been thwarted by our declaration of independence. The man and woman retreat to their second line of defense when they hear the one who has given them life and blessed them; they hide among the trees of the garden.

God's question, "Where are you?" (v. 9), can carry several shades of meaning. It is certainly not a request for information; God knows where the man is, and the man is aware that he cannot really hide from God. He answers immediately, and he answers the question that is really being asked: "Why are you hiding?" He admits his fear of his Creator. Why fear? Because he expects the death penalty to be inflicted? He does not say that; he is afraid because he is naked, defenseless, and feeling the need for defense. God has not changed, but the human has, and from his position of independence God now looks different, threatening. The question, "Where are you?" is heard as an accusation. But from God's side the question may have another overtone, and that is grief. For "Where are you?" can be a grieving question. If the story is to have its proper effect on us, we ought to see ourselves there among the trees. That is, we ought to recognize our own pitiful defenses thrown up to attempt to justify ourselves against a God of whom we are not quite sure, and then perhaps also be presented with a revelation. On the other side, the relationship has not been broken off completely, for it is maintained by a sorrowing God.

God's second question, "Who told you that you were naked?" (v. 11), is also not a request for information. There was only one possible way to produce the man's present condition, and that was not by anyone telling him anything. It could only have happened as a result of violating the one limit that God had placed on human freedom. So God does not wait for an impossible answer but moves directly to the point. The conversation is getting more forceful now, for in Hebrew "Did you eat?" comes at the very end of the sentence, for emphasis. In the man's answer we learn (or are reminded) that the effort to become independent produces not only insecurity but also an inability to bear responsibility for its negative results (v. 12). The force of the man's defense can only be represented in English by underlining: "The *woman* whom thou gavest to be with me, *she* gave me fruit of the tree, and I ate." He ate, but there are two others to blame for it. Our author was obviously a keen observer of human behavior, and in a few words has represented in classic form innumerable feeble defenses. Who among us has not attempted one of them? The woman is still fully equal, for she is now given her chance to accept responsibility as the LORD asks her, "What is this that you have done?" (v. 13). And she remains equal to the man, in her guilt, for like him she can do no better than find someone to blame, the serpent. So the discussion ends. No interrogation of the serpent is necessary, for the harm that has been done has been done to the two humans, who had been intended for a special relationship with God and have rejected it. There is no devil to blame for it; for what is wrong in this world, between person and person, people and their God, is the direct result of the human act of self-assertion, attempting to determine good for themselves over against the source of all that is truly good. Human life in alienation, incompleteness, and fear is the direct result of our insistence on denying our absolute dependence on God. There are innumerable aftereffects of that desire to be on our own, as the subsequent verses will remind us.

INDEPENDENCE CONFIRMED: COMPLETENESS DISRUPTED (3:14-24)

The Real World: Snakes (3:14-15)

The author now describes reality as we all know it, and makes it the consequence of the human inability to accept absolute dependence on God. Our relationship with God, which was the center of vv. 1-13, now falls into the background; it is the absence of harmony between men and women, humans and the natural world that is now the subject. Real snakes are obviously the subject of v. 14, and an etiology is provided for two of their peculiarities, that they can move very well indeed without legs and that they eat dust (as people of antiquity thought). A curse is put upon the snake, one of only three curses uttered by God in the entire OT (also v. 17; 4:11). The preposition following this curse, translated "more than" (RSV "above all"), was taken by Jewish interpreters to mean that even in the last days snakes would not be blessed as would other animals. This may account for the odd statement in Isa. 65:25, which asserts that even in the ideal world of the future, when God makes everything right, there will apparently be one exception: "dust shall be the serpent's food." But the preposition may mean "apart from," rather than "more than"; if taken that way it puts a kind of ban on serpents, separating them from the rest of living creatures.

Although Gen. 3:14 can only refer to real snakes, Christian interpreters have regularly insisted that v. 15 changes the subject and refers to the devil, promising his defeat by the Messiah. This protevangelium (literally, "first messianic promise") appears first in the writings of Irenaeus (ca. A.D. 130-200), and it has been defended by many writers to this day; but it has also been rejected by such early authorities as Chrysostom, Augustine, and Jerome, as well as most modern scholars. This interpretation is actually a classic example of poor exegesis since it insists on a change of subject between vv. 14 and 15 that is not supported by the text, and it introduces a promise in the midst of vv. 14-19, which otherwise deal entirely with punishment. It tries to find a decisive difference in the two, very similar actions that are described (bruise your head, bruise his heel) and tries to force the collective noun, "seed," to bear a singular meaning, so as to refer to only one of Eve's offspring, the Messiah. Long ago, John Calvin already understood these two verses correctly, writing of the first, "I interpret this simply to mean that there should always be the hostile strife between the human race and serpents, which is now apparent; for, by a secret feeling of nature, man abhors them." A recent survey of the attitudes of eighty thousand British children (ages four-fourteen) toward various animals has corroborated Calvin's opinion; to a remarkable degree, the snake dominated their list of dislikes. The reasons for these extreme aversions are still not altogether clear, but evidence does show that this animal was a natural choice for the role given it in Gen. 3. The hostility described in v. 15 may include a tacit reference to all the hostilities that now exist between humans and animals, however; and if so, it provides some of the background for Israel's hope that in the world to come God will do away with all hurting and destroying (Isa. 11:6-9).

As for the effort to find a messianic promise here, Calvin wrote that he would like to agree with those who take the seed to be Christ, but that "seed" is "too violently distorted by them; for who will concede that a collective noun is to be understood of one man only?"

The Real World: Women (3:16)

The focus of this verse is the major distinction between women and men, the ability to bear children. Woman's glory, the ability to bring forth new life, is in the real world only possible through great travail. The OT authors, most of whom were probably men, were obviously deeply impressed by the pain their wives experienced in childbearing, for they frequently refer to it. But women do not attempt to avoid this pain: "your desire shall be for your husband." The man's desire for his wife had been alluded to much earlier, in 2:24, for it does not involve quite the same ambiguity. The woman's continuing desire for her husband despite the resulting travail of pregnancy and childbirth is more appropriately mentioned here, in the context of the ambiguities of life in the real world.

Her desire for her husband also continues in spite of all that is wrong with male-female relationships in the real world. Only in a world perverted by self-assertion, by the claim to personal autonomy, by the loss of harmony among humans and God, does the man rule over the woman. That this is the result of human sin and not the will of God was recognized by early interpreters. But unfortunately many of them were so heavily influenced by their culture that they tended to accept it as the unchangeable order of the present time, ignoring the NT message that in Christ the restoration of equality between male and female has already begun (Gal. 3:28; note that "Be subject to one another out of reverence for Christ" takes precedence over "Wives, be subject to your husbands" in Eph. 5:21-33).

The Real World: Men (3:17-19)

No curse is uttered against humans, but the serpent (Gen. 3:14) and now the ground are cursed (v. 17). Human sin is represented as introducing into the world a kind of contagion or pollution that affects all of nature. The ground, from which humans themselves were made and which could, in the story, nourish the beautiful fruit trees of Eden, produces adequate food for people only through the most strenuous and unending exertion. Moreover, in the midst of a continuing battle against thorns and thistles, it produces vegetation that does not nourish and that threatens the growth of the useful plants (vv. 17b-19a). The curse that human sin has brought upon nature rebounds against the humans, for they are dependent for their welfare on nature's health and peace. In earlier years of the scientific era these old Israelite ideas of the unity of human welfare and the welfare of nature sounded rather primitive; but environmental studies (prodded by environmental disasters!) have begun to teach us that the material world is more than a stage on which history is played out and a source of raw materials for us. The OT teaching that nature also needs redemption, because of the effects of human sin upon it, may no longer seem merely a primitive notion, but takes on a relevance that we have too long been able to ignore (cf. Isa. 24:1-13, 17-23; Rom. 8:19-23; Col. 1:15-20).

Work, which God intends to be a part of his blessing of humanity (Gen. 2:15), is too often a curse in the real world because of its futility, of the uncertainty of its results, of the drudgery that often brings forth little of value. The OT elsewhere expresses the hope of the redemption of work, in the last days (e.g., Isa. 65:21-23; Zech. 8:10-12). And death is the inevitable end of the struggle to maintain life (Gen. 3:19b). Often these words have been taken as the pronouncement of the death penalty, against which the human was warned in 2:17; but many scholars believe that death is here depicted as the eventual release from toil, and not necessarily as a punishment. In these words (3:16-19) man and woman are not condemned to death, but to life. They must go on, separated from God, the source of blessing; but existence spent far from God is existence on its way to death.

Out of Eden (3:20-24)

The man is still *ha'adam* ("the human"); he is called *ish* ("man") only in vv. 6 and 16 of this chapter, where the word specifically means "husband." He now gives his wife, however, a proper name, *hawwah*, a word that resembles the Hebrew word for life. The name is explained by referring to her as the mother of all life, a probable reference to her child-bearing ability, which was the focus of v. 16. The name was transliterated as Eua in Greek and became Eva in Latin, from which we get Eve in English. The woman has a name, but the ambiguity of *adam* continues into ch. 5; her male partner is still just a "human." Perhaps it seemed appropriate for the female to be called something analogous: "life."

We are nearing the end of the first in a sequence of stories that recounts human failure and divine response, running from ch. 3 through ch. 11. The divine response in each of these stories will be seen to be twofold. Punishment must come, for God is just; and the punishments for these primordial sins represent the realities of the world in which Israel lived, and which they attributed to sin, not to the divine intention for life. But there is always an element of grace in these stories, acts of divine mercy that preserve humans from the worst consequences of their rebellion. Two elements of grace may be noted in the concluding verses. People now exist as isolated entities over against one another because of their declarations of independence, and they need defenses to exist. God acknowledges that, and in 3:21 provides usable clothes to replace the first pitiful efforts at protection. The OT understands that we cannot save ourselves, cannot find ways to return to the Edenic state simply by becoming nudists or vegetarians. Clothing itself may serve as a reminder that we are saved by grace alone.

The expulsion from Eden is also a mixture of judgment and grace. God himself acknowledges that the serpent was right in saying, "you will be like God" (v. 5), for now he says, "Behold, the man has become like one of us, knowing good and evil" (v. 22). The first person plural appears again (as in 1:26; cf. Isa. 6:8), and among the several theories (see above, 27) I prefer the reference to the heavenly court, although it is perhaps not so satisfactory here as elsewhere. Something must be done about this divine likeness in humanity, for they have become self-conscious individuals, knowing that they can make autonomous decisions; but they are not wise enough, good enough, or strong enough to make right decisions. Their likeness to gods gives them instead the capability to introduce immense suffering into the world; and if they could live forever, the suffering would become infinite. So the death of this would-be god is not solely punishment for hybris; it is also a blessing, delivering the god and those around from the great harm that is now potential. So Eden is revealed to be no real part of human experience; it represents what ought to be, but is a place we do not know and cannot reach. The cherubim, which usually function as guardian spirits in the OT and the ancient Near East, separate the world of Eden from our real world. Man and woman live east of Eden, in a world of enmity, pain, drudgery, and death.

CAIN AND HIS FAMILY

Genesis 4:1-26

The story of Cain and Abel is one of the best known in the Bible, for despite its difficulties it speaks of a subject that everyone understands: rivalry and dissension within families. Certainly not every family has experienced hatred and violence in its midst, but it is unlikely that there has existed any intimate human relationship where some envy and some anger have not appeared. Our experience of those emotions provides an immediate point of contact with the tragedy of Cain and his brother. This is another of those "sagas" or "archetypal stories" that are far more important for what they say to us about ourselves than for any information they may convey about individuals who lived long ago.

The story probably had a long life of its own before it was taken up by J and made a part of his account of how human life began. Although it has been carefully connected with the story of the first man and woman in the garden, and is more loosely connected with chs. 5 and 6, several obvious discontinuities remain that evidently did not bother J as much as they have distressed later readers. J knew that the story would be most effective in this location, even though it did not fit perfectly.

Here, in brief, are the problems of continuity. After the birth of the two sons (4:1-2) Adam and Eve disappear from the story of what should have been a family tragedy and do not reappear until v. 25, when another son is born. The story itself completely ignores the existence of a father and mother, unlike other stories of sibling rivalries in Genesis (cf. 27:5-46). Then Cain, after being condemned for killing Abel, fears that "whoever finds me will slay me" (4:14). Who are these other people that he fears, and where did he find a wife (v. 17), not to mention citizens to populate the city he builds? The whole chapter (except for vv. 1-2, 25) seems to presuppose a different background from that provided by chs. 2–3, one in which Cain and Abel live in an already well-populated world. Furthermore, the genealogy at the end, leading to the founding of guilds of cattle-raisers, musicians, and metallurgists, seems strangely irrelevant when we realize that all the descendants of these people will be wiped out by the Flood. Originally, then, the story of Cain and Abel was probably told as a self-contained narrative, without having any relationship to the stories of the garden or the Flood. We shall need to think about its impact as an isolated story, and also try to appreciate its contribution to the continuous narrative of how things began that now forms Gen. 1–11.

The Genre—Accounting for Unanswered Questions

This is a tantalizing story because so much has been left unsaid. Every interpreter has felt it necessary to fill in the gaps, to answer questions the story raises but leaves undiscussed. How did the brothers know they were supposed to bring offerings to the LORD? What was acceptable about Abel and his offering and unacceptable about Cain and his? What did Cain say to Abel? ("Let us go out to the field" is not in the original Hebrew of 4:8.) Why did not Cain receive the death penalty for murder? What was the protective mark that the LORD put upon him?

Is it a poorly told story, since it leaves so much unsaid? I suggest that if that were true it could not have had so profound an effect on the imaginations and consciences of generations of readers. It has been told with care and skill in the concise, highly selective way that was typical of Hebrew story telling, although this may be one of the more extreme examples of selectivity. The verse-by-verse discussion will attempt to show how effectively this conciseness has made it a universal story, rather than merely a reminiscence of two unfortunate young men who lived long ago. It will be argued that what has been left out is a key to what is important; that is, we ought not to bother ourselves overmuch about sacrifice or about whether the Kenites were tattooed, since the author does not want to discuss those subjects. And there are ample clues, an abundance of emphases that tell us what really interested J as he made this traditional story a part of his work.

Concerning Cain and Abel we know only their occupations and that they brought offerings to the LORD. Certainly this means J recognized that their character and previous relationships were not essential to the purpose of his story. Neither did it matter why Cain's offering was rejected. The center of the narrative consists of dialogue between God and Cain concerning the latter's treatment of his brother and its effect on the relationship between Cain and God. In vv. 8-11 is a striking cluster of words that ought to alert us that we have reached the center of the story and to provide the key to its interpretation. In those four verses the word "brother" occurs six times; the first three times seem unnecessary, for they are used along with the name Abel. We already know the two are brothers; why are we reminded of it so insistently? The center of this story is the murder of a brother, and the way J has told it—with his emphases and his omissions—ought to lead us to consider the awfulness, indeed the irrationality of such an act, an act that is the archetype of the worst of the violence that human beings continue to inflict on one another.

Cain and His Family as Part of the Primeval Story

The psychological background of the story is certainly the universal problem of sibling rivalry, and this associates it with a large number of other stories, in the OT and in world literature, which develop the same theme. But that is background, as the story now functions. The sociological background is also familiar to us, for it is the long-standing rivalry between herders and farmers. That is even less significant, however, for the story's present meaning. A third possible background has been much discussed, that it originally dealt with the early history of the Kenites, that interesting tribe with which Israel usually had friendly relationships, since they seem to have been worshippers of Yahweh (Gen. 15:19; Num. 24:21; Judg. 1:16; 4:11-17; 5:24; 1 Sam. 15:6; 27:10; 30:29; 1 Chr. 2:55). In its Hebrew spelling the word Cain could well be the origin of the tribal name, and it is possible that this chapter does contain some early traditions about those people; but once again, in its present form the intention of this account is quite different.

The structure of Gen. 4 is provided by a genealogy, which begins in vv. 1-2 and makes the connection with chs. 2–3. It is interrupted by the story of Cain and Abel in 4:3-16, then continues through seven generations in vv. 17-22 until it is interrupted by the Song of Lamech in vv. 23-24. The chapter concludes with a fragment of another genealogy recording the births of Seth and his son Enosh.

The genealogy provides continuity between the originally separately existing stories of the garden, the two brothers, and the Flood. Eventually J will come to materials that make it possible to write something like a history, as he follows the sons of Jacob into Egypt, into bondage there, and later out into the wilderness. The kinds of materials preserved for him did not make it quite possible to write a full-fledged history of these early periods (with careful chronological information and cause-effect relationships spelled out). That very thing was being done for his own time, however, by the author of the so-called Succession history of David (2 Sam. 11–1 Kgs. 2). We can see the influence of such historical thinking on J's work, even in Gen. 2–11, where his materials contain no precise chronological information at all. In addition to the genealogical materials, he found another way to associate this story with ch. 3, by choosing a series of terms that echo the account of the rebellion against God: "know" in 3:5, 7, 22 and 4:1, 9; "till" in 3:23 and 4:2, 12; "keep" (or "guard") in 3:24 and 4:9; "drive out" in 3:24 and 4:14; "ground" in 3:17, 19, 23 and 4:2, 3, 10, 11, 12, 14. Several of the same phrases occur in both chapters, also: "Where are you?"/"Where is your brother?", "What have you done?", "Cursed are you", "East of Eden." The end of 3:16 is an interesting variation on 4:7.

The story of Cain's crime thus continues several themes introduced in ch. 3, especially estrangement from the ground and from one's God. It also introduces a theme that had only been alluded to in several ways in the preceding story, the devastating effects of estrangement from fellow human beings. The climax of each story also contains the same theme, the mixture of judgment and grace with which God responds to these appalling human failings; that theme will reappear in the stories of the Flood and the tower of Babel. The interest in the growth of human culture that is contained in the genealogy at the end of the chapter also has some ties with the account of city building in that latter story. Despite the discontinuities noted earlier, we can see that these materials have been skillfully used in order to develop several ongoing themes, and these are the subjects that will draw the most attention in the interpretation that follows.

The Brothers Are Born (4:1-2)

The connection between chs. 3 and 4 is not smooth. All we know is that the human was driven out of the garden to till the ground. No indication is given of where the couple went or how they began a new life; the next we hear of them is that they had intercourse and a child was conceived. This abruptness is easier to understand when we realize that 4:1 uses the standard formula of genealogies, so it represents the introduction of an entirely new genre and is not the direct continuation of the story of the expulsion of the man and woman from the garden. We are told nothing of the life of Adam and Eve after 3:23 ("to till the ground from which he was taken"), except that they became parents. They appear in 4:1-2 only to provide an introduction to the story of Cain and Abel. As in ch. 3, Eve is the speaker, naming Cain with one of the most cryptic explanations in the Bible. The verb she uses normally means "buy," or more generally "get." Six times (in poetry) it has the meaning "create," with God as subject. Some take the sentence as her cry of pride at the discovery that she could produce life: "I have created a man as well as the LORD." The statement involves a play on words between the verb *(qanah)* and the name Cain *(qayin)*, but exactly what Eve meant by it cannot be determined. The word translated "with the help of" in the RSV and "as well as" in the translation given above ordinarily simply means "with." Since the story makes no further reference to Eve's saying, we are left with nothing better than guesses; apparently the interpretation of the name was not of great importance to J. Abel's name is not interpreted at all, but it comes from a word meaning "breath, nothingness." Since Abel plays no active role in the story, gets no lines at all, and dies early without offspring, the name may well have been supplied by early tellers of the story, indicating his fate in advance.

The two brothers are immediately identified as representative figures: Cain of the farmer and Abel of the herder. Two rival lifestyles involving ways of producing food that have often come into conflict with one another are thus said to have existed virtually from the beginning. The inhabitants of the land of Canaan were well-acquainted with this issue, for seminomadic tribes with an economy dependent on sheep and goats often encroached on their farmland. The conflicts resulting from these two types of food production have continued into modern times in the American West, as commemorated in the song from the Rodgers and Hammerstein musical *Oklahoma!,* "The Farmer and the Cowman (Should Be Friends)." Those two rivals both scorned the sheepherder. But note that this can scarcely be taken as the major theme of the story, since neither party fares very well. The sheepherder dies and the farmer is uprooted from his land, and the issues are deeper than sociological conflicts.

Cain's Dilemma (4:3-7)

The story moves very rapidly, with a minimum of detail. The introduction to v. 3, "In the course of time" (Hebrew "At the end of days"), drops us into some undefined point in their lives when both bring to the LORD offerings of produce from their work. It does not matter to J whether they had done this before or why it was done at this time. He and his original audience would simply have assumed it was the natural thing to do; everyone made offerings to their gods, and no commandments instituting or regulating sacrifice are found in the stories of early days, throughout Genesis. Neither does he explain why God treats Cain and Abel differently.

This has produced a tremendous amount of discussion, with two approaches predominating. Most interpreters insist on finding a moral lesson. The author of Hebrews claims it was because Abel offered his sacrifice by faith (Heb. 11:4). Others point to the words "firstlings" and "fat portions," deducing that Abel brought of his best, while Cain's offering was something nondescript. An effort to read later sacrificial theory back into the story has also been made, claiming Cain's offering was unacceptable because it did not involve the shedding of blood; but this is very dubious, since offerings of fruit and grain were a regular part of later sacrifices (e.g., Exod. 23:19; Deut. 26:2).

A second approach admits the story itself is not explicit either about the nature of the gifts or the attitude of the givers, and takes the incident to be an example of God's freedom to elect or reject whom he wishes, citing Exod. 33:19: "I will be gracious to whom I will be gracious."

I propose a third approach, taking J's disinterest in the act of sacrifice itself as a clue that he really intended us to see this as only one example of a problem that occurs frequently in human life, that of unexplainable inequality. Two persons seem equally qualified; one finds work and the other does not. One takes good care of health and gets a severe illness; another breaks all the rules and leads a healthy life. One finds love and friendship from companions; another must struggle daily with unpleasant people. The examples could be multiplied without end. And the reactions vary greatly. I believe the issue raised in Gen. 4:3-7 is precisely the question of how one reacts to the inequalities of life. Some do not ask why but just put up with inequalities as best they can. Others attribute them to luck or fate and may curse their luck. But some see their lot as a matter of injustice and are inclined to blame God for their lack of success. The anger that may result, either from blaming luck or blaming God, has the potential of being directed against society in general or certain favored individuals specifically.

"Cain was very angry, and his countenance (or 'face') fell." Since the story is told of an offering to God that was not accepted, the author draws us into the minds of those who blame God for their troubles. The LORD'S questioning puts the issue directly before those people: Will you let injustice destroy you? (Recall his question to Jonah: "Do you do well to be angry?" Jonah 4:4, 9). Cain is given an option; he need not interpret life that way. If he does well, or as we might say, if he focuses instead on the good he can find in life, then he can lift up his face (Gen. 4:7). The RSV translation, "will you not be accepted?" is probably not an accurate rendering of the single Hebrew word that appears here. Literally it means "lift up," and it is the same verb used with "countenance" to indicate a favorable disposition in Num. 6:26. Since we have just been told that Cain's "face fell" in v. 5, indicating his anger, it is very likely that the Hebrew expression "lift up" in v. 7 indicates the possibility of a change of attitude.

Then comes the warning. The reaction of resentment and anger because of life's unexplainable inequalities will lead to sin, which will destroy both self and others. As we find elsewhere in Scripture, God does not justify himself or explain the mysteries of the apparent injustice and irrationality of life when he is challenged to do so (cf. Jer. 12:1-6 and the books of Job and Habakkuk). Often his initial response is to remind the complainer that there is something that person can do about it, something more useful than blaming God, and he adds the promise of a blessing to those who persevere, even when life does not make much sense (Jer. 15:15-21; Hab. 2:4; cf. Hab. 3:17-18). The mystery remains, however; and just as we encountered a puzzling sentence in Gen. 1:2, where cosmic evil somehow had to be acknowledged, and a puzzling character in the appearance of the serpent, when temptation became the subject, now we encounter in 4:7 words that have been called the most difficult sentence in Genesis. I suggest the words defy certain understanding because they deal with that subject that defies understanding: the existence of sin and evil. The most likely translation seems to be one that nearly personifies sin—something the OT is ordinarily reluctant to do—and reads, "Sin is the demon at the door, whose urge is toward you; yet you can be his master" (Ephraim A. Speiser, *Genesis*, 29, 32-33). The challenge then is this: Cain and we have the option of dwelling on life's unfairness, blaming it on God, and thus allowing it to separate us from God and leave us victims to the power of sin. But Cain and we have another option: accepting what comes and trying to make the best of it, with God's help. The story says God did not accept Cain or his offering, adopting the position of those who believe themselves to be mistreated by God; but the story goes on to insist that God is still there, attempting dialogue with Cain (note that Cain does not answer). God offers a better way—a denial of environmental determinism that says we must be what our experiences make of us. He insists that it is not what happens to us but how we react to what happens that determines the kind of people we become. And God challenges every inclination to blame misfortune on him, for he is there with Cain, trying to help.

Murder (4:8-12)

As the story is told, it is God with whom Cain has the problem. Nothing is said about Abel ever doing anything to harm Cain. It was God who did not accept Cain's offering—so Cain killed Abel. What good did he think it would do him? Was it just because he hated Abel for faring better than he? Did he think that with Abel out of the way he could make a better impression on God? Does any explanation make sense?

Of course it does not. The strangeness, the disjointed character of vv. 7-8 represents very accurately the absurdity of sin. God has addressed Cain with a warning and an offer, but set forth in what is to us very cryptic language. Cain makes no answer to God, but instead says something to his brother; we do not know what. The Hebrew text baffles us by giving an introduction to a direct quotation in v. 8a, then breaking off without a speech. Early translators felt the need to supply something and added, "Let us go out to the field"; but this does not appear in any Hebrew manuscript. Instead we are confronted immediately by a murder scene. And in every clause we are reminded: They are brothers. The insistent reminder, "his brother," "your brother," must be a commentary on the absurdity of the human predicament, that it is not only strangers who hate and kill one another; for those who are closest to one another often find it impossible to avoid doing incalculable harm to each other. Claus Westermann comments, "What is so shocking about the whole event is that a man like him, who does his work and presents his offering to God, is capable of this. It is not Cain, but everyone who can become the murderer of one's brother" (*Genesis 1–11*, 302). And 1 John uses the Sermon on the Mount as a basis for commenting on this story when it announces, "Any one who hates his brother is a murderer" (1 John 3:15; cf. vv. 11-18 and Matt. 5:21-24).

When God asked of Adam, "Where are you?" (Gen. 3:9), the human's sense of estrangement led him to respond immediately with a defense. But when God asks of Cain, "Where is Abel your brother?" the killer responds first with a lie, "I do not know," then with an insolent counterquestion: "Am I my brother's keeper?" The answer (despite homiletical statements to the contrary) must be, "Of course not." Abel was a free human being, he did not need a "keeper," and no one is expected to be continually aware of the whereabouts of another adult who is mentally and physically able.

None of us is to be the keeper of our adult brothers and sisters; that is patronizing and demeaning. But the question as Cain asks it is only an attempted diversionary tactic; it is part of the lie, and so the LORD properly ignores it.

As with Eve (3:13), the LORD'S next question to Cain calls for self-condemnation: "What have you done?" No defense will suffice, for the murder victim himself has testified: "The voice of your brother's blood is crying to me from the ground." In the OT life itself is equated with blood (9:4; Lev. 17:11, 14), and the special treatment of the blood of animals slain for sacrifice or simply for meat (e.g., Lev. 1:5; 17:1-14; Deut. 12:20-28; 1 Sam. 14:31-34) was intended to remind Israelites that the lives they were taking were God's possession. If even the lives of animals were so important to God, then the unlawful taking of a human life introduced an awesome irregularity into the world that had to be set right. As yet there were no laws against killing, but that would not seem anachronistic to the Israelites. The shed blood, the violently taken life, would require recompense—with or without law.

God responds to a cry for help such as the oppressed on earth raise to him (e.g., Exod. 3:7, 9; Job 19:7; Ps. 77:1; Isa. 5:7), but this time it comes from shed blood, which to Israel seemed to loose a destructive force in the world that had to be dealt with somehow (e.g., Deut. 21:1-9; Jer. 26:15; Ezek. 35:6). The OT, in which so much killing is reported (for it simply records what really happens in human affairs), is a book that reveals a great uneasiness in the soul of Israel concerning the taking of life. That uneasiness is expressed in powerful terms in this account of the first murder. Within ten verses we have encountered the first human production of life, with Cain's birth, and the first human destruction of life, carried out by Cain.

The shed blood has polluted the ground that has received it (Gen. 4:10), not in some magical sense, but because murder has introduced a curse into the world, even as Cain's parents' sin had done (3:17). That curse will now rebound against him, even as we have found that the violence wreaked by our societies has made the world a threatening place for us. So Cain receives a curse that will separate him from the ground, the original source of his livelihood. The expression "cursed from the ground" probably means separation from it as a source of life, as vv. 11 and 14 indicate. Cain is the only human being cursed by God, but even so, he does not have to pay for murder by being executed. Despite the regular use of the death penalty for murder in Israel (9:5-6; Exod. 21:12; Deut. 19:4-13), in this account of the first murder God does not take life in recompense for the shed blood; indeed, he will shortly take special measures to preserve it (Gen. 4:14-15).

Cain will be banished from the realm of normal life, however, (v. 12). He is to become a displaced person, "a vagrant and a vagabond," as G. A. F. Knight represents the Hebrew wordplay. As his parents had been banished from Eden, Cain must now exist on the fringes of the life-giving world—still existing, but cut off from abundant life by the power of his brother's life that he had spilled upon the ground. Could this also be an archetypal experience? At the end of this chapter, after having fully traced the fortunes of Cain's family, I will suggest that it is.

Judgment and Mercy (4:13-16)

Cain speaks twice in this story, and his second response to God has been interpreted in two ways. Jerome, Augustine, Martin Luther, and others have taken his first sentence to mean, "My sin is too great to be forgiven," and Augustine corrected him, affirming "God's mercy is greater than the misery of all sinners." English translations read, "My punishment is greater than I can bear." The difference is due to the ambiguity of two of the three words in the Hebrew sentence. Hebrew *'awon* may be translated either "sin" or "punishment," for it includes within itself the whole range, from the sinful act through the resulting guilt to the consequent punishment. Its existence in Hebrew helps to show that Israelites did not think of punishment as a more or less arbitrary or optional thing, but saw sin, guilt, and punishment as inevitably connected. Hebrew *nasa* means "to lift up," and as such can be used with *'awon* as a metaphor for "forgive" (e.g., Lev. 10:17; Ps. 32:5; Isa. 33:24). But it also means "to bear" or "carry," and in this sense is used with *'awon* for enduring the consequences of sin (e.g., Ezek. 4:4; cf. Isa. 53:12). From what we can learn of the character of Cain, we must conclude the earlier interpreters were on the wrong track. No suggestion occurs anywhere in the story of confession, repentance, or forgiveness, so this sentence can hardly be taken as an acknowledgment of sin or guilt; it is only a complaint.

Cain thus represents unrepentant humanity as he continues on his earlier course of blaming God for all that goes wrong. He has rejected the option that God had offered him (Gen. 4:7), and with that he has rejected God. Even Cain is not so blind that he cannot recognize that life and blessing come from God, so it is no comfort to him to say "from thy face I shall be hidden," as we might think.

No longer will he live, as Hebrew understands life, but he will exist. Mere existence is still preferable to death, however, as his concluding words indicate (v. 14). Having killed, he now fears being killed; what he could inflict on his brother is more than he himself can bear.

It was not the NT that first taught that God loves the unlovable. Cain is scarcely an endearing character, moving as he has from anger to violence to resentment, yet God's judgment upon him is mixed with mercy (v. 15). It is not God's intention that one killing should produce more. He uses the oath of a family avenger of blood (Judg. 8:18-21; 2 Sam. 2:22-23; 3:26-30; 2 Kgs. 14:5), but here as a guardian who intends to prevent bloodshed rather than as an executioner. The mark that God placed upon Cain is clearly protective in purpose and not the mark of a curse, as some have misunderstood it. We are given not one clue as to the nature of the mark, and much time has been wasted on pure speculation as to what it might have been; indeed, since nothing suggests that anyone but Cain has ever borne it, the question is completely irrelevant. Its only meaning as the story is told is as a sign of God's grace, even grace toward the archetype of violent mistreatment of one's brothers and sisters. Here as elsewhere we are assured that even in the midst of God's just judgment of our sins he intervenes to save us from the worst possible consequences we might bring upon ourselves.

The so-called "land of Nod" (Gen. 4:16) in which Cain is said to have dwelt, "away from the presence of the LORD," is no specific country at all, for *nod* is simply another form of the word translated "wanderer" in v. 12. It may thus mean the desert, the place where nomads wander; at any rate, Cain is to exist there separated from the blessings of God. Like his parents before him, his fate is not to die, but to have to go on living.

Cain's Family and the Beginnings of Civilization (4:17-24)

Between the stories of Cain and Abel and the Flood are three genealogical notes plus the brief reference to the origin of the Nephilim in 6:1-4. The genealogies leave many questions unanswered. The first (4:17-24) follows Cain's descendants down to the seventh generation after Adam. The second (vv. 25-26) begins over again with Adam and Eve, recording the birth of another son Seth, and their grandson Enosh. Chapter 5 starts over with the births of Seth and Enosh; then comes a list of names much like those in 4:17-24, except for variations in spelling and the interchange of two names.

Gen. 5	Gen. 4:25-26
Adam	Adam
Seth	Seth
Enosh	Enosh
	Gen. 4:17-22
Kenan	Cain
Mahalel	Enoch
Jared	Irad
Enoch	Mehujael
Methuselah	Methushael
Lamech	Lamech
Noah	Jabal, Jubal, Tubal-cain, Naamah

Chapter 5 shows every sign of belonging to the P source, and it provides a clear connection between ch. 1 and P's version of the Flood. It is generally assumed that the genealogies at the end of ch. 4 belong to J, but their origin and function are much debated. It has been suggested there were originally two Cains, the farmer about whom the story was written and the city builder of the genealogy; but this does not solve the problem of the three lists of names, and is probably a solution to a nonexistent difficulty. Farmer and city builder need not belong to different traditions in antiquity, since most of the population of ancient Palestinian cities were farmers who worked the surrounding land. Neither is the apparent nomadism of Cain after the murder incongruent with his reputation as city builder, for it might be a reference to the caravan cities built in oases far out in the desert, such as Palmyra and Tema.

However, two traditions probably arose concerning who was the first child of Adam and Eve, contained in two slightly different genealogies. One began with Cain, the other with Seth; but the family trees recorded were essentially the same after that, including Lamech as the final entry. If so, J may have used the Cain tradition because it contained notes concerning the beginnings of human culture that were of more than antiquarian interest to him. When J and P were combined, it is likely that 4:25-26a were added in order to account for the apparent discrepancy, making Seth the third child, not the first.

Many creation stories in world literature account for the beginnings of human culture; here we have only a few brief notes. Horticulture has been a part of human life since the very beginning, according to 2:15. The domestication of animals is first associated with Abel (4:2); but since he died without issue, the credit is later given to one of Lamech's sons, Jabal (v. 20). Jubal is said to have been the originator of music making (v. 21), and Tubal-cain was the first metallurgist (v. 22). As for Lamech's daughter Naamah, she is mentioned but we do not know why. Perhaps something has been lost. Agriculture, art, and technology have been summarized in the briefest possible form, and we must not forget that the ancestor of all these guilds is Cain, the builder of the first city. The genealogy does not end with Lamech's children, however, but with the citation of an old war song attributed to him (vv. 23-24). That is highly significant. It reveals a streak of increasing violence running alongside all these important human accomplishments. The Song of Lamech completes Cain's story with the return to killing.

Adam's Family Continued (4:25-26)

Cain the murderer, the city builder, the father of civilization, is not to be the ancestor of the rest of humanity, as the story is now told. His genealogy is broken off by the announcement of the birth of another child to Adam and Eve. His name is Seth, and the name of his son is Enosh, an old Hebrew word meaning "man." This helps to explain the fragmentary new family tree at the end of Cain's story. Enosh can be a virtual synonym for Adam, so in effect the human race is starting over.

With Enosh is also associated the time when "men began to call upon the name of the LORD." This verse (v. 26) has been frequently cited in source critical work because it seems to represent J's theory of when the name Yahweh was first used in history. According to the E source the name was first revealed to Moses on Mt. Horeb (Exod. 3:13-15), and P has a similar account located in Egypt (Exod. 6:2-3). In Genesis E and P ordinarily use Elohim rather than Yahweh, in accordance with their theory; but J uses Yahweh from the very beginning, and Gen. 4:26 seems to correspond fairly well with that. The correspondence may not be perfect, for Eve has already used the name in v. 1, long before the time of her grandson Enosh. This may be explained, however, by the more precise meaning of "call on the name." As Gen. 12:8; 13:4; 21:33; 26:25; etc. indicate, it means to worship Yahweh, not merely to use his name. So this note probably corresponds to some extent to those concerning Lamech's sons in the previous genealogy, in that it speaks of another aspect of human culture, the beginning of religion.

Reflections on Genesis 4

The serpent promised, "You shall be as gods," and God acknowledged that did happen: "Behold, the man has become like one of us" (3:5, 22). Chapter 4 begins to explain what that means. Human beings are able to create life (v. 1) and to destroy it (v. 8). They are beginning to demonstrate their mastery over the world, by domesticating animals, learning to work metal, and to make music. They have begun to fill the earth and subdue it, as the genealogies and the scattering of Cain's family demonstrate. Their most important work, the true beginnings of civilization, is mentioned, though only in passing: Cain built a city (v. 17). It is surely one of the ironies of the chapter that the first murderer builds the first city. We should not make too much of that, as Jacques Ellul did in making it the key to a negative judgment of the city throughout the Scriptures (*The Meaning of the City* [Grand Rapids: Wm. B. Eerdmans, 1970]), for the Bible usually depicts the city in positive terms. People of antiquity understood far better than we that civilization and the existence of the city are coterminous. We who can live in comfort in rural areas do not easily understand the brutish nature of village life in early times. Of course the concentration of power in the city made possible new forms of suffering, so the biblical picture is ambiguous, as we shall see more clearly in 11:1-9. Still, we must not forget that in both Testaments the new heaven and new earth are depicted in the form of a city, the New Jerusalem (Isa. 65:17-25; Rev. 21:1–22:5). But that will be a city without the violence of the one who killed his brother or of his descendant who threatened vengeance seventy-seven fold.

We have also added to our understanding of the knowledge of good and evil, which humanity gained through its declaration of independence from God. For the first man and woman that act yielded shame and fear (Gen. 3:7-10). For Cain, who reaffirms the declaration, it leads first to envy and anger, next violence, and finally wandering. Now let us return to the question asked in connection with 4:12-14, whether Cain the fugitive and wanderer is in any respect an archetype of widespread human experience. Indeed, he is the first displaced person; but the genealogy contributes something more to his portrait. He has children, builds a city, and becomes the father of civilization—yet he is the perennially alienated person, fearing "whoever finds me will slay me." Who are the fugitives and wanderers today, the perennially alienated? Not only the refugees, the nomads, the gypsies, but also city dwellers! Those living in comfort in the country need not congratulate themselves because of that remark, for they too are the victims of the ambiguity of civilized life. Cain is the classic example of the truth that we can and do accomplish marvelous things, but that all of it is corrupted by that estrangement from God (3:8-10; 4:14) which makes us killers of our brothers and sisters. The gospel in this truth is that the same God who justly punishes our violence toward one another also protects us from the worst we could do to ourselves if that independence we seek could really become complete.

FROM ADAM TO NOAH
Genesis 5:1-32

Many people in modern cultures are interested in genealogies; but that is largely a private matter, tracing one's own family tree in order to develop a sense of one's personal history. In other cultures genealogies may perform more public functions, in addition to being of private interest. Recent studies have identified two types of traditional genealogies: the linear, in which only one offspring of each individual is listed (cf. Gen. 4:17-18; 5:1-31), and the segmented, which shows how various branches of a family are related. The beginnings of segmentation appear in 4:19-22; 5:32, and Gen. 10 is a full example of the type. The linear type has some obvious uses in traditional societies, such as to legitimate one's right to kingship or to the priesthood; and it still performs a meaningful function for those who trace their family trees hoping to be able to take pride in being descended from some famous person. The segmented type is important politically in traditional cultures, in that what modern societies would call diplomatic relations have in the past regularly been authenticated by showing that families, clans, or tribes have a common ancestor. This type will be discussed more fully in connection with Gen. 10, which shows how all the nations are descended from Noah through his sons Shem, Ham, and Japheth.

We do not know what the original use of the genealogy in Gen. 5 may have been, but we can find some clues both to a historical and a theological use as it stands in its present context. The whole chapter (except possibly part of the description of the birth of Noah) clearly belongs to the P source. Direct connections are evident between vv. 1-3 and 1:27-28. The term translated "generations" reappears in a series of genealogies that provide the structure of P's work, from Adam to Aaron (6:9-10; 10:1-32; 11:10-26, 27; 25:12-16, 19-20; 36:1-5, 9-43; 37:1-2; Num. 3:1-3). This shows that for P genealogies have become a valuable resource for his historical interests; they provide elements of chronology and hold events and periods together by their record of a sequence of births.

The discovery of lists of Mesopotamian kings, with a break in the

FROM EDEN TO BABEL

Genesis

lists for the great flood described in the Gilgamesh Epic (see the Commentary on chs. 6–8), has led to a great deal of speculation about possible relationships between the genealogies in Gen. 5 and 11 and those lists. The first documents of that kind to be studied recorded ten kings before the flood; Gen. 5 lists ten generations before the flood. The antediluvian Mesopotamian kings were given fantastically long reigns, from 18,600 to 43,200 years, while the reigns of the kings after the flood were much shorter. A similar shortening of life span occurs in Genesis, from 777-969 years in ch. 5 to 148-600 years in ch. 11. At one time it was thought that some of the names in Gen. 5 could be derived from the Mesopotamian king list. However, new discoveries and reconsiderations have led to more caution in drawing parallels.

The antediluvian names in the king lists are Sumerian, and have no demonstrable connection with those in the Bible. More recently discovered lists have seven, eight, or nine kings before the flood, rather than ten, showing that ten generations is not such a fixed pattern as was thought. Furthermore, the Mesopotamian texts are not genealogies but lists of kings who ruled in various cities, and no blood relationship among them is suggested. What holds the lists together is an ideology of kingship that "descended from heaven" and was claimed to have passed from one dominant city to another. So, despite certain similarities, the biblical and Mesopotamian texts are quite different from one another.

It does not help us much to observe that the 900-plus life spans of Adam and his immediate descendants are comparatively reasonable when set alongside purported reigns of 36,000 years and more in the king lists, for Gen. 5 is still off by a factor of about ten, as we know human life. One could cite a half dozen ingenious mathematical schemes attempting to explain the numbers in this chapter; but none of them has attracted many followers, so we remain without an adequate explanation of the long life spans. The most conservative interpreters claim that the diseases that now shorten human life did not yet exist before the Flood, so these numbers can and should be taken literally; but we have no evidence to confirm this theory. Many consider the numbers to be examples of the common tendency to idealize the past, thinking that the world is getting continually worse; but if that was P's point of view, he nowhere states it explicitly, as later writers did. (Cf. Hesiod's ages of gold, silver, bronze, and iron; and the prediction in Jub. 23 that in the future the world will grow so corrupt that a three-week-old infant will look like a one-hundred-year-old man!) The numbers, plus the lack of detail about most of those mentioned and the unique description of Enoch, serve to separate us from any sense of kinship with the characters in this chapter. We have in common with them birth, begetting, and death, but everything else in the chapter makes them belong to a world different from ours. The genealogies are often criticized for being dull, but Gen. 5 is not so much dull as it is incomprehensible, for unlike most of the Bible it speaks of things we know nothing about.

The chapter can be seen, however, to have served an important purpose for P. The first three verses show his intention to trace the blessing bestowed at creation down to the present; and that is of considerable significance for his theology, given that optimism we noted in Gen. 1. The next major body of narrative material P wishes to use is the Flood story, but tradition did not associate it directly with creation. So the genealogy provides a way to connect the two, while the long life spans provide an appropriate time interval between the two great primordial events.

P's Creation Story Continued (5:1-5)

Just as P continues the Flood story with a genealogy in Gen. 10, so ch. 5 follows naturally after the conclusion of his Creation story in 2:3. The ambiguity of *adam* is more obvious here than elsewhere. In 5:3 it is the proper name of a man who becomes a father—Adam— but in v. 2 it is the name of the human race, including male and female. The word "man" in vv. 1b, 2 of the RSV is the same word that is given as the proper name Adam in vv. 1a, 3, 4, 5. The confusion is present because the genealogy includes only fathers and their firstborn sons, but the connection that has been made with the creation of humanity in 1:27-28 includes the recollection that *adam* is composed of males and females. If these verses were written by P as he combined his work with the J source (as seems likely), then 5:1-5 serve as a corrective or modification of the impression left by chs. 2–4. The blessing of 1:28 is reiterated (5:2) to show that it has not been completely lost; and creation in God's likeness is recalled so that the significance of the ensuing statement that Adam begot a son in his likeness (after his image) would not be missed. Older interpreters (e.g., John Calvin), who insisted the image of God in man was lost in the fall, say it was Adam's defiled state that was transmitted to Seth and all his posterity. But modern scholars have noted that nowhere does the OT say the image of God in humanity was lost or destroyed. Consequently they believe P is affirming the continuing likeness of humanity to God, despite the sinfulness that J has documented. Some rabbinic interpreters found these verses to be of great theological significance as a declaration of universal human brotherhood. Despite our differences, they said, all human beings have one Creator, the Heavenly Father, and one ancestor, the human father.

Enoch (5:21-24)

Only four verses are devoted to Enoch, but he became a legendary figure of great importance in later Judaism, and Christianity also was much influenced by the Enoch tradition. He appears elsewhere in the OT only in 1 Chr. 1:3, but Sir. 44:16 makes of him "an example of repentance to all generations," evidently drawing on an extrabiblical tradition. Again, Heb. 11:5 paraphrases Gen. 5:24, elaborating that it was "by faith Enoch was taken up so that he should not see death." Details concerning Enoch are added in two retellings of Genesis that we now possess, Jub. 4:16-25 and the fragmentary Genesis Apocryphon from Qumran (2:19-26; 5:3). Two lengthy apocalyptic books were also ascribed to Enoch himself; 1 Enoch (available in full only in Ethiopic) and 2 Enoch (only in Slavonic). Both were originally Jewish works, but 1 Enoch was widely used in the Church through the 4th cent. A.D. and 2 Enoch is now available only in an edition that includes extensive Christian additions. It is not impossible that all this might have come from fanciful exegesis of the cryptic and tantalizing verse, Gen. 5:24; but many scholars think that this verse is only a passing allusion to a larger tradition that already existed in P's time and that probably originated with stories about Enmeduranki, the seventh member of the Mesopotamian king list. Despite his great importance later on, Enoch is a figure of only passing interest for P, however. He is remembered for his special relationship with God; only he and Noah are said to have "walked with God," meaning they lived in a continual, intimate relationship. Only he and Elijah are said to have been "taken" by God. The Elijah story more clearly indicates that Israelites believed some sort of bodily translation into God's presence, without experiencing death, was possible in a few exceptional cases (2 Kgs. 2:1, 9-12). When Israel began to struggle with the question of the relationship of individuals with God after death, two psalmists chose that same common verb "take" in order to affirm their confidence that death could not sever their intimate communion with God, even though at that time they could say nothing more specific about life after death (Ps. 49:15; 73:24). In both cases the RSV reads "receive," but it is the same verb used of Enoch.

The Birth of Noah (5:29, 32)

Lamech's etiology of the name Noah involves a clear reference to Gen. 3:17 and uses the name Yahweh; so 5:29 is often thought to be a fragment of J's genealogy, which broke off before reaching Noah in ch. 4. The meaning of Lamech's saying is not clear. Noah seems to be a form derived from the Hebrew root meaning "rest," but the explanation uses a different root *(nhm)*, meaning "comfort" or "relief" (so RSV). What kind of relief Noah was expected to offer from "our work" and "the toil of our hands" is not indicated, so for lack of anything better scholars have suggested it refers to his reputation as planter of the first vineyard (9:20-21). Nothing in that tradition, however, offers much support to the theory. Lamech's saying does not seem to be a meaningful etiology in terms of what the OT now preserves about Noah.

As the genealogy segments, with reference to the birth of three sons (5:32), Noah's story is interrupted by a brief prelude to the Flood that probably originally belonged to the J source (6:1-8). Then P's account resumes in 6:9 with his familiar formula, "These are the generations." The Hebrew of 5:32 suggests that all three sons were born in Noah's five hundredth year; but the RSV's "After Noah was five hundred years old" is probably the correct interpretation, and we need not think they were triplets.

FRAGMENTS CONCERNING THE TIME BEFORE THE FLOOD

Genesis 6:1-4

For a theological commentary, this is one of the most difficult passages in the Bible. It is not that no one has found the passage theologically significant; quite the contrary, far more theology has very likely been drawn from it than the passage really contains. Early Jewish authors considered it to be more important than the story of the sin of Adam and Eve, for this passage was retold many times while the Eden story is only occasionally alluded to. For several authors this was the true "Fall story," the account of how evil came into the world by means of the descent of certain rebellious angels (e.g., Jub. 5:1-11; 1 En. 6–10, 86–88; 2 En. 18; T.Reuben 5:6). For these earliest extant interpretations there was no question about the identity of the "sons of God": they were fallen angels. Later Jewish and Christian authors "demythologized" the passage, however. Among Jewish writers the sons of God were identified as members of the nobility who married beneath them. Christian authors insisted that the sons of God were the descendants of Seth, while the daughters of men were from the line of Cain. Variants of these interpretations continue to be defended to this day, but the dominant opinion at present is that these verses contain a fragment of a mythological theme well known from ancient sources, in which divine beings ("sons of the gods," as the Hebrew of Gen. 6:2, 4 may be read) cohabited with human women, producing semidivine offspring. Most modern commentators admit that the polytheistic origins of the passage have been only imperfectly disguised by the Israelite author, but the reasons for that have never been adequately explained.

All interpreters, ancient and modern, however, agree that the intent of these four verses is to describe the proliferation of sin on earth and to show that it involves a transgression of limits of some kind— either between the heavenly and earthly realms (angels or divine beings) or the standards set for acceptable human behavior (when the sin is taken as licentiousness). But when the verses are read carefully, without the usual interpretations in mind, it will be seen that none of these themes is present in any integrity here. We encounter one non sequitur after another. The first verse does not follow naturally after anything that precedes; v. 3 connects with neither vv. 2 nor 4; vv. 4a and 4c go together but are interrupted by 4b in a clumsy way; and only 4b has any relationship to v. 2. Moreover, the rest of ch. 6 contains no further reference to any of this. Many have called 6:1-4 a fragment, but it may in fact be three fragments—vv. 1-2, 3, and 4a, c—which originally had little or nothing to do with one another or were associated in a larger context which it is now impossible to reconstruct. In addition to the discontinuities, we are confronted by three unknown words, *yadon* (RSV "abide"), *beshaggam* (RSV "for"), and Nephilim (KJV, TEV "giants"). Finally, although this is regularly taken as a story about the increase of wickedness on earth, these verses contain no explicit word about either sin or punishment!

This leaves one final question, the most important one for a theological commentary: "Why?" These verses have not inappropriately been called a "cracked, erratic boulder"; but even so, they did not appear in this place by accident. Some reason must have existed for putting them here. As we consider the question of continuity between the Flood story and what precedes it (Cain, in J; and the long genealogy, in P), we can see that the two clear beginnings of the Flood story, v. 5 (J) and v. 11 (P) each provide a rather abrupt introduction of worldwide wickedness. J's version (6:5-8) might have come naturally after 4:24, if Noah had been introduced; but P's genealogy in ch. 5 gives no hint of increasing general wickedness. We can see, then, that the context has led virtually every reader to expect 6:1-4 to tell us something about a massive increase of wickedness that corrupted the whole earth, and it has been possible to find such an idea in these fragments. We can imagine better transitions than this, and indeed the interpretations, ancient and modern, all involve a considerable use of the imagination in order to make of these verses a meaningful passage. But frustrating as it is, we must admit it has succeeded in setting the right tone for what follows.

The Sons of the Gods and the Daughters of Men (6:1-2)

The first verse seems innocent enough and clear enough, compared with the rest, but when examined closely it is an extremely vague introduction. "When humanity *(ha'adam)* began to multiply" presumably should refer back to the beginnings of the genealogies, to the immediate offspring of Adam and Eve rather than to a time as late as that of Noah. The statement "daughters were born to them" is a strange one, for there would have been no multiplication beyond the first generation without daughters. Certainly it can be taken as a meaningful statement only as an introduction to the next verse. Scholars have detected here an allusion to the mythological theme of "the overcrowded earth," but must admit it serves no purpose in this context.

The debate over the identity of the "sons of God" or "sons of the gods" has already been alluded to. The Hebrew can be legitimately translated either way, and the OT does occasionally refer to "gods" (e.g., Ps. 82); so the decision will depend on how close to the surface we think the author intended the mythological background of his material to appear. Most interpretations do not allow any hint of polytheistic thought. We have seen that at first the "sons" were called angels, and later they were regarded as completely human figures, the descendants of Seth. These were the two main choices until modern scholarship found an abundance of ancient myths recounting the sexual union of gods with human beings, increasing the probability that these verses do allude to some such myth that would have been known to the Israelites. But scholarship has also discovered the widespread tendency to ascribe deity of some sort to kings in the ancient East, and this has offered a new version of the old human identification. It is claimed that the verses refer to the accumulation of harems by kings who may have been referred to as "son of god." A great deal has been written about licentiousness and about the improper use of power to satisfy one's lust; and the offspring of these unions have been called "bastards," although the text says they "took wives." When we simply read the words of the text, however, we find no explicit statements about licentiousness or power. Perhaps more theology (or moralizing) has been found here than really exists. We shall reconsider this when we get to v. 4.

God Speaks (6:3)

What we can detect of a pattern in these verses seems to correspond to that which has already appeared in chs. 3 and 4: sin followed by judgment, with the full effects of guilt mitigated by divine grace. If that pattern does exist here, it would be clearer if 6:3 and 4 were reversed in order, however, for there is no clear reason or reference for the LORD'S words in v. 3 as it now stands. Thus far it has never been intimated that the LORD intended his spirit to abide in man forever, so the nature of the change is not clear, and neither is the reason. Accordingly, much discussion has focused on the word *ruah* ("spirit"); but the most natural reading, understanding *ruah* to be the life principle animating human beings (2:7), seems most likely. Since the verb used with it is an unknown word, the RSV translation "abide" is only a guess. Half a dozen possible derivations have been suggested, but all remain merely guesses. The word introducing "he is flesh" is by general agreement now translated "since" or "for," but it also remains questionable. In addition, the meaning of the 120 years remains subject to debate; is this now to be the maximum life span, or does it represent the interval before the Flood comes? The natural reading would take it as a limitation of the human life span ("for he is flesh"); but since in the succeeding chapters many individuals are said to have lived longer than this, the interval theory has been proposed as an alternate. It is a virtually meaningless reading, however, for nothing is said that would explain the reason for such an interval between this event and the Flood.

In short, we cannot be certain of anything in this verse, but it does seems most likely to be a divine limitation of human life to a 120-year maximum. What that has to do with 6:1-2, 4 remains a subject for the imagination to explain. Assuming that the actions of v. 2 represent a sin on the part of the sons of the gods, we are left with no punishment of them mentioned. Do the 120 years then represent an unexplained punishment of humanity, or do they apply only to the offspring of the unnatural union? Any explanation is guesswork.

Giants in the Earth (6:4)

The structure of this verse is very awkward. Presumably it intends to say that the Nephilim were the offspring produced by the union of divine and human parents, but that could have been done in a more straightforward way. The Nephilim in v. 4a appear to be identified with the mighty men of old in v. 4c, with v. 4b the apparent continuation of v. 2. Scholars generally agree that v. 4a is a gloss, intended to identify the mighty men of the original story with the people known to have lived in the Hebron area before the Israelite occupation of the land (Num. 13:33). This produces, however, a strange anachronism: we are in the primeval era, before the Flood; but the Nephilim and Anakim of Numbers, in addition to the Emim, Rephaim, and Zamzummim who are associated with the Anakim, are all connected with Canaan, Moab, and Ammon during the period just before the "Conquest." All are remembered for their great height (cf. Deut. 2:10-11, 20-21; 9:2), but no hint is given in any other biblical references that they were thought to have had a supernatural origin of any kind. Perhaps, then, Gen. 6:4a, c was a note concerning mighty men of old, of gigantic stature, and it is v. 4b that is the gloss, mistakenly and rather clumsily attributing their origin to a union of sons of gods and daughters of men? If so, one begins to think that v. 3 is also a fragment originally unconnected with either of these themes.

We expect every verse—or at least every paragraph—of Scripture to have some meaning for us, and as a result few commentators have reached such negative conclusions about these verses as I have. But is it not so that when we read just the words that are there, they do not in fact say very much? No doubt their origin can be traced to myths of divine-human sexual encounters and legends about giants in the earth. The theology of J—sin, punishment, mitigation— seems to be detectable here, but in no clear form. The need of some such paragraph at this point in the completed narrative can be recognized, however; and perhaps at one time it existed in a form more strongly mythological than later readers, editors, or copyists could permit, so that as a result it has become hopelessly truncated. It is tempting to interpret this as another piece like Gen. 1:2 and 4:7, where the reason for the difficulty of the language is the impossibility of the subject—the existence of evil in a world created and ruled by a good God. But it seems wise not to build too much theology on a text that is as unclear as this one.

NOAH AND THE FLOOD

Genesis 6:5–8:22

This is one of the best-known stories in the Bible. Indeed, even people who are largely ignorant of Scripture know something about Noah, his ark, and the great Flood, for the story has captured the imagination in a remarkable way. Yet when we compare it with the stories of Eden, of Cain, or of the tower of Babel we must admit that it is not an equally impressive job of story telling. We find in Gen. 6–8 no intriguing characters such as Eve or Cain, and there is not even any dialogue to enliven the story. God speaks several times, but Noah gets no lines. Noah's virtues are listed and emphasized for us, but he never quite materializes as a fully-rounded human being. In spite of this, however, readers and interpreters of the story have regularly supplied for Noah the human qualities that the words of the story omit, and have felt the pathos that *must have* been present in that family's experiences, even though it is ignored in the text. Something about this story has captured the imagination of all kinds of people, and we shall see that its appeal is due in part to the way it is told; but what makes it of special interest to the interpreter is that it also fascinates in spite of the way it is told.

The subject is a terrifying event—a worldwide catastrophe destroying almost every living thing—but it is told in a very restrained, almost matter-of-fact way. For an example of how a Hebrew author might have described such an event in a highly dramatic way, compare Ps. 18:7-19 or Hab. 3:3-15. By contrast our imaginations are given only a few clues concerning the emotional impact of the great Flood (Gen. 7:11-12, 17-23), and the storyteller concentrates instead on rather prosaic details: the construction of the ark, the animals that were saved, and how long it all took. We shall see that the clues that have been provided have been sufficient to capture the imagination, however. The narrator's decision to emphasize the ark rather than the drama of storm and destruction will be seen not to be the result of his inability to tell a story effectively, but the result of an important theological choice. The story of the Flood is told not to emphasize the truth that God must judge the wickedness that corrupts his good earth, but in order to present the gospel that in the midst of judgment it is God's primary intention to save his people.

The Story

Martin Luther obviously had a good sense of the art of Hebrew narrative, for he felt something unusual about the Flood story. In his Genesis commentary he remarks several times about the repetitious nature of what he found. This was long before anyone had thought to explain this as the combination of two sources, so Luther offered an explanation of his own: "It is obvious that God enjoys talking to Noah. It is not enough for Him to have given him orders once about what he should do, but He repeats the same orders in the same words" (on 7:2). Here are some examples of the problem Luther and others have encountered: In 6:14-21 Noah is instructed to make an ark and load it with animals and food, then we are informed (with emphasis) that Noah did just as God commanded him (v. 22). Presumably they are all on board, but the very next section repeats the instructions (with variations) and once again we are told Noah obeyed (7:1-5). Twice is not enough, however, for they all enter the ark again in vv. 7-9 and once more in vv. 13-16. The first two sections are good examples of what source analysis calls "doublets," two versions of the same thing. The differences between the two accounts of boarding the ark also have provided clues for the identification of two originally separate sources. For example, 6:14-22 uses the word Elohim ("God"), and specifies only two of each kind of animal, while 7:1-5 uses Yahweh and speaks of seven pairs of clean animals and one pair of unclean. Another major problem in the story that has been resolved by dividing it into two sources is its chronology. Does the Flood last 40 days (7:17) or 150 days (v. 24) or a year (compare v. 11 and 8:13)? This is not the place to discuss all the evidence for the division into sources or the continuing debate over its correctness. That material is conveniently presented in the commentaries by John Skinner and Claus Westermann. We shall work with the generally accepted analysis, considering along the way the distinctiveness of J and of P, but will use the present, combined form of the story as the basis for our work since it preserves a clear structure; and in spite of the repetitions and contradictions that do exist, the present form of the story has its own message that is the result of the combination of the two original sources.

The introductions and conclusions of the two sources, in which their most distinctive contributions are found, were preserved in blocks by the redactor. But the central portions, the accounts of the

Flood itself, were apparently so much alike that they were inter-woven, obviously following a very conservative principle of keeping virtually everything from both sources, even though that produced considerable repetition. Here is the generally accepted division of the story.

	J	P
God's Decision	6:5-8	6:9-13
Construction of the Ark		6:14-22
Entry into the Ark	7:1-5, 7-8, 10	7:6, 9
The Flood	7:12, 16b, 17, 22-23	7:11, 13-16a, 18-21, 24
The End of the Flood	8:2b, 3a, 6-12	8:1-2a, 3b-5, 13a
Exit from the Ark	8:13b	8:14-19
Sacrifice and Promise	8:20-22	

P's conclusion (9:1-17) also includes a promise, but is otherwise completely different from 8:20-22.

The Reality of the Flood

Until the science of geology began to develop in the 19th cent., it was generally assumed that the Flood was a literal account of the destruction of all life except for one human family and for pairs of each kind of earth animal. It was believed to be an event that occurred only a few thousand years ago. Both geology and archaeology have the potential for supplying visible evidence of such a flood, but not only have all archaeological excavations failed to uncover any such evidence among human habitations, the record of the earth's history discovered by geology virtually rules out the possibility that anything of that sort has ever happened. Given what we now know about the earth, it is very doubtful that the world-engulfing Flood described in Genesis was ever a physical reality. But there is more than one kind of reality!

The Geological Evidence

Early excavations in lower Mesopotamia found thick levels of silt separating occupation levels of several ancient cities, and at first it was thought this might be evidence for Noah's Flood. But later careful comparisons showed that these floods occurred at different times, so they had to be called local inundations. No evidence indicates massive flood levels encompassing more than a very small part of the earth in historic times. Certainly, geology does show that extensive flooding of what are now the continents occurred more than once in early eras, but all of this activity occurred long before the appearance of human beings on earth. Even during those periods marked by a great deal less land surface than exists today, there is no evidence that the whole surface of the earth was ever covered by water at the same time.

During human history the shape of the earth's surface has changed very little; the highest mountains today look very much the same as they did when civilization began in Mesopotamia and Egypt in the 3rd millennium B.C. This means that a flood deep enough to have covered the highest mountains (the Himalayas) would have required more water than now exists all told in the atmosphere, the ice caps, and the oceans. We might respond that God simply miraculously provided all that water, then removed it; but those who still insist that the Genesis Flood must be read as a literal, physical event are fond of a pseudoscientific suggestion. They hypothesize that until the time of Noah the earth's atmosphere was enveloped in a heavy blanket of moisture, which was suddenly precipitated, as told in Gen. 7:11. This is only a theory, however, with no evidence for such an envelope or for what could have become of all that moisture after the Flood.

This pseudoscientific approach also proposes to explain the fossils by claiming that they were all deposited at the same time and that the wave action of the Flood somehow sorted them neatly into the various strata in which they lie separated now. All the strata were deposited by the Flood, and the violent movement of the water somehow also sculptured nearly all the present topography of the earth. But such an idea has its foundation only in one theory of the inspiration of Scripture, which claims that since the NT refers to the Flood a physical event exactly as described in Genesis must have occurred—or else Scripture lies. Therefore, because of a theory concerning inspiration it becomes necessary for these people to produce another theory that violates all that geology has learned about the natural processes of rock and land formation. Perhaps it is the theory that is wrong, and it is fully possible for us to accept (as I do) the inspiration of Scripture without having to deny the testimony that the earth presents in various ways. For there are other kinds of reality.

Evidence from the History of Religions

Another type of evidence exists that might be used to support the belief that a worldwide flood once occurred. The folklore of many cultures includes a story about a flood of one sort or another and an explanation of how a few people and animals were saved. The basic story is so widespread that the abridged edition of Sir James G. Frazer's *Folk-lore in the OT* contains ninety-seven pages of summaries of the various plots. The material is not evenly distributed around the world; Frazer found virtually no trace of flood stories in Africa, nor in central or eastern Asia. But its bulk still leads one to ask whether any better explanation exists for the reappearance of a theme in such widely diverse cultures than to propose, as does Gerhard von Rad, that it requires "the assumption of an actual cosmic experience and a primitive recollection" of it (*Genesis,* 124). Might it be that far back in the prehistoric era there was such massive and widespread flooding across the inhabited areas of the earth that it left a folk memory preserved until this day in a great variety of forms— that is, a prehistoric rather than a historic Great Flood? Another option is that an original, local flood story has been transmitted from its source to far off regions, where it has taken on local color over the centuries.

For the ancient Near East there is clear evidence that a certain flood story was transmitted from one group to another. The Gilgamesh Epic contains a lengthy account of a flood from which only one man and his wife were saved; and it contains details, such as the sending out of the birds and the sacrifice at the end, which are remarkably similar to Noah's story. Another Akkadian epic, Atrahasis, also tells about a great flood; it has fewer close parallels to Genesis, but occurs in a similar context, connecting the flood with the account of creation. Neither Atrahasis nor Gilgamesh represent the original context for this episode, but each uses an already existing tale for its own purposes, as the discoveries of fragments of earlier Sumerian versions show. These Mesopotamian texts are evidence for the transmission of a very popular story from century to century and from people to people; among the recipients of this tradition were the Greeks (Deucalion) and the Hebrews (Noah). Each people used the flood story for its own purposes, however, and we shall see that the theology of Gen. 6–8 is radically different from that of its nearest parallel, Gilgamesh.

Once we recognize that both J and P were using traditional material, a story that was no doubt already well-known to their readers in one form or another, we are led toward the answer to the question of what kind of reality this story represents. As we try to understand the contribution of the Flood to the continuity of Gen. 1–11, we shall see that in several respects it does not seem to fit very well. Both J and P have made explicit additions and interpretations in order to make it fit as well as they can. But we may ask, if that was necessary, why did they use it at all? A suggested answer comes from the History of Religions approach and a reconsideration of the prevalence of water imagery in religion, in addition to the appearance of flood stories the world over.

The prevalence of flood stories is less adequately explained by the hypothesis of folk memory of an early, worldwide deluge than by a hypothesis based on the symbolic power of water. (See M. Eliade, *Patterns in Comparative Religion,* 188-215; *The Sacred and the Profane,* 129-136.) Water is the most potent symbol of chaos, for in itself it has no form, all other forms are swallowed up and disappear in it, and it engulfs and extinguishes life. It is suggested that experience of floods of local extent, along with the personal awareness of the terror of drowning, are the factors largely responsible for the appearance of flood stories in many cultures. The potency of water as a symbol for the threat to all ordered life—the danger of the inbreaking of chaos—also may account for the popularity of these stories and may explain why Noah is one of the best-known biblical characters. From time to time, well-ordered lives and stable communities are threatened by disaster, by a change for the worse so awful that chaos seems to be lurking at the edges of controlled, meaningful existence. And water continues to provide the most effective imagery for expressing those feelings. We use the Greek word "cataclysm" of the worst disasters, a word that originally meant "deluge." We speak of the feeling of being inundated, deluged, engulfed, overwhelmed. We talk of barely keeping our heads above water and of sink-or-swim situations. The flood—and specifically Noah's Flood, in cultures influenced by the Bible—has become another of those archetypal experiences of which this book has spoken earlier.

We can now understand better why both J and P used the Flood tradition as part of their primeval history, for it is a truly primeval experience in the universality of its appearances and impact. It was a tradition that already had a power of its own among the people, and as such it has continued to have an immediate point of contact even with those who know little or nothing about the unique message of Scripture. But as the story now appears, enriched by the combined theologies of J and P, it functions also at another level, making a unique contribution as a statement concerning Yahweh's dealings with a world threatened by chaos.

God's Decision (6:5-13)

Without warning God and the readers of Genesis are confronted by a world that has grown totally corrupt, with the exception of one man. Up until now we have read of the occurrence of specific, individual sins (chs. 3–4) and have been made aware of some undefinable threat of evil (1:2; 3:1; 4:7; 6:1-4), but have been given no preparation for God's sweeping condemnation of "all flesh" in 6:13. The sources (J, 6:5-8; P, vv. 9-13) agree that the situation is hopeless, though they describe it in different ways. This is one of the most important sections in the story, for it contains nothing taken from common Near Eastern flood traditions. Here we find the unique interpretation of the Flood created by the religion of Israel. Unlike any other flood story, Gen. 6–8 makes it an act of judgment against evil, pronounced by the God of righteousness.

J had before him a Flood tradition that spoke of the destruction of the whole world, except for one man and his family, as a result of a divine decision. Given his understanding of God, he could use such a story only by making it a righteous judgment, so that all humanity would have to be guilty. He has not quite prepared us for that; but we have already seen evidence that J is pessimistic about human potential, so what he now says is at least in general agreement with what has preceded. In the stories of Eden and of Cain and Abel he had found a way to show how divine grace prevails even in the midst of judgment, and the Flood tradition must have been appealing to him because the story of how one family was saved from the Deluge could be used to develop that same theme at length. So at the beginning J justifies God and goes beyond that to describe the divine pathos in the midst of judgment. This then helps us to appreciate more fully why the bulk of the story deals with the fact and the means of salvation.

J has written of sinful acts before, but now dares to comment on what is in the human heart and, even more daringly, what is in the divine heart. He ascribes emotions to God and records a divine soliloquy in order to leave no doubt that the blame for this awful destruction lies on human wickedness. He also leaves no doubt about how such an act of judgment affects God. Here is no impassive, sovereign judge, enforcing the law without feeling; here is no vengeful sovereign seeking to assuage hurt feelings. J's choice of words in these four verses is significant. The extent of the problem is emphasized by speaking now of a condition, rather than of specific acts (the same word, *ra'ah/ra'*, is first translated "wickedness" and then "evil" by the RSV in v. 5). The hopelessness of that condition is expressed by a cluster of words in this same verse: "great," "every," "only," "continually." So J justifies Yahweh's decision. Then the contrast between God and humanity is brought home by speaking of two hearts: "every imagination of the thoughts of his heart was only evil continually" (v. 5) is set over against "and it grieved him to his heart" (v. 6). God's lamentation, expressed as a divine soliloquy, follows (v. 7). The verb form translated "was sorry" (*nhm,* niphal) is used thirty times of God and only six times of humans. In twenty-four of those uses it refers to God changing his mind, in spite of 1 Sam. 15:29, which insists that he never does that. In seventeen of those cases, in keeping with his character, God decides not to inflict the judgment originally planned. Twice (here and in 1 Sam. 15) he regrets a previous act, intended for good, which has gone wrong because of sin. The mystery of how human free will could apparently overrule the divine intention is not answered; the author's only concern is to tell us how this affects God. This first verb reveals that God is truly involved in human affairs and is affected by them to the extent that he does change. The second verb *('atsab),* translated "grieved" in Gen. 6:6, elsewhere means "displeasure" or "pain." It is significant that J uses it here of God, for two other forms of the root were used to designate woman's pain in childbirth in 3:16, and one of those forms is also used of the man's hard labor in 3:17. Now God experiences the same feelings (also used of God in Ps. 78:40; Isa. 63:10). Until recently Christian orthodoxy felt a serious problem with these attributions of emotion to God. John Calvin employed the concept of "accommodation" here; according to Calvin, these verbs do not properly belong to God, but since we cannot comprehend him as he is such statements are accommodations to our limited capacity. Martin Luther would not even accept that, and insisted such emotions could only be attributed to human beings, God's ministers (in this case, Noah). Today, however, there is a much wider readiness to accept the sometimes startling biblical testimonies to the true personality of the Divine Person, and to dare to speak of the suffering of God.

It is with divine grief, then, that Yahweh says, "I will blot out man whom I have created" (Gen. 6:7). This verb, *mhh,* is another key word for J's theology of the Flood. It is a strong word meaning "to wipe out" or "wipe away," that is, "to do away with" completely. Its thoroughness is alluded to in 2 Kgs. 21:13. The verb is used in two very different ways: of complete destruction of a person or group (Deut. 9:14; Judg. 21:17) and of forgiveness of sin (Ps. 51:1, 9; Isa. 43:25; 44:22). In the Flood story, sin results in thorough destruction; but the two ways this word was used in Hebrew may have left a question in the minds of Israelites, a question still left in the air at the end of the story. God will promise no wholesale destruction again (Gen. 8:21-22; 9:11, 15), but nothing is said yet about how he will

deal with continuing human sinfulness. Evidently it is too early to
speak of forgiveness in the primeval history; but attentive Israelites,
noticing that *mhh* is used four times in the early part of this story
(6:7; 7:4; twice in v. 23), might well realize with gratitude that in
their present existence "wipe away, blot out" is what God promises
to do with their sins.

P begins with Noah, the righteous man, connecting the Flood
directly with the genealogy of ch. 5 by means of 6:9-10. The following verses parallel J's introduction but speak of earth and all flesh instead of humanity. This makes a clear connection with 1:31, where
God declared that everything he had made was good; now we are
faced with the shocking word that it is all corrupted. Behind this may
lie P's veiled acknowledgement in 1:2 of some unexplainable evil in
the cosmos that is normally kept completely under control by God.
If so, then P found in the Flood tradition a way to speak of the
human dread of chaos in terms that would not contradict his Yahwistic theology. Somehow, without explanation, God's good world has
become "corrupt," using a word that means both "to corrupt" and
"to destroy," so that in 6:13 he can use the same verb of what God
intends to do to that world. It is a corruption like rust or rot, which
destroys as it transforms, so that God's word of judgment might be
understood as simply the divine verification of the fact that the destructive effects of violence (v. 13) are inevitable.

P speaks of corruption of the whole creation, in distinction from
J's emphasis on human wickedness; but the two accounts are not
contradictory, for both recognize that all living things are bound up
together in a common destiny. P's account allows for the possibility
of nonhuman evil; but the only evil we have any control over is
human sin, so it is important that the introduction to the Flood
begins with J's emphasis on human responsibility, acknowledging
that it affects the welfare of the rest of the world (v. 7).

Boarding the Ark (6:14–7:9)

The first part of this section is the continuation of a block of P material that includes 6:9-22. Only P gives any information about the
construction of the ark (in vv. 14-16); in J's account Noah is just told
to enter it (7:1). Most commentators think J's version of building
the ark was omitted when the two sources were combined; but since
the editor seems to have been so conservative in preserving dupli-
cates in the rest of the story, we might also consider the possibility
that for J the ark was a divinely provided means of salvation.

The ark was made of an unknown wood, *gopher*, mentioned only here in the OT. Several guesses have been made; a good candidate would be cypress, which is water resistant and was used for boats in antiquity. The shape was that of a long shallow box, about 135 meters (440 feet) long, 22 meters (75 feet) wide, and 13 meters (45 feet) high. John Calvin may have noticed that it would have been roughly the shape of a coffin, for he comments on what a trial it was for Noah to "forsake the world, that he may live in a sepulchre," seeking "a new mode of life in the abyss of death" (commentary on 7:1). Noah is told to build this enormous structure in a perfectly matter-of-fact way, with no hint of awe at its size and none of the comments about the magnitude of the task that abound in later literature. How one man could do this and also gather the animals and the food required for them all (6:21) has been a matter for repeated discussion, but it was not a subject of interest to P. The salvation of a portion of the earth's living things is primarily an act of God's will, for both J and P, and the one thing about Noah that is important to report is that he obeyed (v. 22; 7:5, 16).

After the description of the ark come sections of P and J material that parallel one another closely. God's plan to destroy all life on earth is revealed to Noah in 6:17 (P) and 7:4 (J), Noah and his family are instructed to board the ark in 6:18 (P) and 7:1 (J), provision is made for saving pairs of animals in 6:19-20 (P) and 7:2-3 (J), and each account ends by reporting that Noah did as God commanded him (P, 6:22; J, 7:5). The word "covenant" appears for the first time in the Bible in 6:18 (P), and its content here seems to be God's intention to save Noah and those who go with him, expressed in a command that Noah obeys. The number of animals to be saved varies in the two accounts probably because J assumed the distinction between clean and unclean extended from creation, while P attributes its origin to the giving of the law on Mt. Sinai. The latter part of this section becomes very repetitious, in order to include both J's use of the traditional time periods (seven days between the order and the rainfall; forty days and nights of rain) and P's introduction of Noah's age as a basis for a chronology of the Flood.

The Flood (7:10-24)

The Creation account in Gen. 1 explained how God made a place for land creatures by separating the waters above the earth from those below the earth (on the second day) and by gathering the waters into seas (on the third day) so that dry land might appear. Those fundamental, creative acts were temporarily annulled, according to P's description of the Flood in 7:11. The authors of Scripture must reckon with the possibility of creation itself being undone, of chaos overcoming order—not because of the popularity of flood stories in their culture but because of the existential reality represented by the terror lurking just beneath this description, a terror that comes to light whenever all that is dependable threatens to break down. But the biblical authors firmly resist the temptation to magnify the terror represented in vv. 21-23 by elaborating on the storm and the scene of death. Having described the beginning of the Flood (P, v. 11; J, vv. 10, 12), the present form of the story repeats yet again the list of passengers (P, vv. 13-16a), effectively reducing the tension. However, the effect of vv. 17-24 remains frightening enough if we visualize it, as so many interpreters have done.

Valiant efforts have been made to resolve the chronological problems of the story. Did the Flood last 40 days (v. 17) or 150 days (v. 24), or should we add them or make the 150 include the 40, and how are these numbers included in the "year" of 8:13? For these questions other commentaries must be consulted, since theories on chronology will add nothing to our understanding of the theology of the Flood.

We have reached the turning point of the story with 7:23b and 8:1. God can and may decide to destroy his created work, but he does so for no arbitrary reason. If he allows chaos to appear again, it is because human lives have already descended into chaos. But even then he does not permit his purpose to be thwarted, for he insists on finding someone to save, on providing a means of salvation, and on preserving a world in which the remnant may live (by continuing animal life). Chaos may prevail only for a while; between "only Noah was left" and "but God remembered Noah" is that interval when nothing happens: "And the waters prevailed upon the earth a hundred and fifty days."

The End of the Flood (8:1-12)

The midpoint of the story is to be found in 8:1: "But God remembered Noah." For God to remember, in Hebrew, does not suggest that he had forgotten anything. It is the signal that he has determined the proper time has come for him to act. After the Hebrews in Egypt had suffered in bondage and cried out for help, "God remembered his covenant with Abraham, with Isaac, and with Jacob," and he called Moses to become his agent of liberation (Exod. 2:24). Even though Israel's continual neglect of the covenant would one day lead to exile and the loss of everything, yet in God's memory there remains the possibility of a future (Lev. 26:40-45). When we con-

sider how undependable our human memories are and how often
"forgetting" is used as an excuse for not having done what should
have been done, we may better appreciate the use of the word "remember" to designate God's patience and faithfulness through the
thin and dark times as he waits for the right moment to act once
again in his graciousness.

The oneness of the fate of all who inhabit the earth is once again
brought to our attention in 8:1, as it has been earlier (6:13, 19; 7:21-
23). For God remembered not only Noah, that righteous man, but
also "all the beasts and all the cattle that were with him in the ark."

Just as the combination of sources produced a slow-moving story
in 6:17–7:16, with Noah's entrance into the ark and the initiation of
the Flood mentioned three or four times, so also it seems the waters
recede in very uncertain stages in 8:3-14 (cf. vv. 3b, 5, 13, 14). The
word *(hsr)* that the RSV translates "had abated" in v. 3 ordinarily
means "to have nothing left," so the reader would think at first that
the Flood was completely over at that point. The lodging of the ark
on a mountain is only the beginning of an extended process,
however, partly the result of the combination of sources and partly
due to J's use of a familiar flood tradition concerning the sending out
of birds. These verses are very closely paralleled by lines 131-154 of
Tablet XI of the Gilgamesh Epic. The effect is to increase the sense
of tension as statements that the Flood is over are repeatedly modified to indicate that it is not yet safe to leave the ark. It had come to
rest on the *mountains* of Ararat. This was the name of a region, not
a mountain (cf. 2 Kgs. 19:37 = Isa. 37:38; Jer. 51:27); cuneiform
records provide information about the kingdom of Urartu (the same
name), which was located in Armenia in the region of Lake Van. The
present Mt. Ararat is so named because it is the highest point in this
region, but there is little reason to think that remnants of the ark
might be found on that mountain. As early as the Reformation period both Martin Luther and John Calvin were wise enough to dis-
miss that tradition, which they found in the writings of Josephus, as
unlikely and of little importance. The Bible indicates only a region,
not a particular peak; furthermore, we have already seen how unlikely it is that any flood ever covered the top of the present Mt.
Ararat.

Exit from the Ark (8:13-19)

According to P's chronology, the Flood lasted one year, give or take
a few days (depending on the calendar being used; cf. 7:11; 8:13-
14). We are to assume that no deaths occurred among the pairs that

entered the ark, for God's intention was to preserve each species. He now repeats the command/blessing of 1:22, 28 to be fruitful and multiply. So life begins anew on an earth purged of wickedness. The blessing will be continued, modified, and expanded by P, with further reference to Gen. 1, in 9:1-19.

Sacrifice and Promise (8:20-22)

The conclusion of J's Flood story uses traditions concerning a sacrifice that also appear in the Gilgamesh Epic (XI.155-196). This is one of the cases where the difference in the way common traditions were used by different authors shows emphatically the contrast between the religion of Israel and that of neighboring cultures. In Gilgamesh sacrifice is the food of the gods, and they are so hungry after the flood that they swarm like flies around it. Genesis provides no hint that Yahweh *needs* sacrifice, but J has preserved elements of the ancient sacrificial tradition here to the extent that God is said to be pleased by it. Some commentators think the purpose was expiatory, to appease any residual anger that might be expended on Noah; but this seems unlikely, given the theology of the Flood story and the theology of sacrifice in the OT. It is much more likely to have been thought of as a thanksgiving offering. Since J has Noah save seven pairs of clean animals, the offering can be made without the loss of any species.

As J provided a potent theological introduction to the Flood in 6:5-8, so he offers a profound conclusion in 8:21b-22, again in the form of a divine soliloquy. The Flood has cleansed the earth (so it can be used as a type of baptism in 1 Pet. 3:18-22), and a new start can be made with one righteous man and his family. But the Flood has done nothing to change the human heart. In Hebrew thought the heart was not so much the seat of emotion as of the rational will; so when God says, "the imagination of man's heart is evil from his youth," it means that the ability and will to do right is missing. Must we, then, expect periodic, wholesale purgings like the Flood? The answer is that this is not the way God works in history. The Flood is an archetypal experience, representing the threat of inbreaking chaos that individuals and societies experience from time to time. But the gospel in the OT Flood story is that the threat of chaos is always under God's control and that he does not use it as the means to accomplish his will. "Neither will I ever again destroy every living creature." There is no hint as yet what God will do about the human predicament; but an emphatic assurance concerning the continuing stability of the present, created order concludes J's story of the Flood (Gen. 8:22).

Reflections on the Theology of the Flood

This is the only narrative in Gen. 1–11 that deals with a righteous man, so it cannot follow exactly the same pattern as the others. Still, it has clearly been told so as to make it a development of J's theme of sin-punishment-grace that appears in Gen. 3, 4, and 11:1-9. The other stories follow a pattern of human initiative followed by divine reaction, but the Flood reduces human initiative to a verse or two and develops the divine response at great length. It also makes saving grace a major theme running throughout the story. This leaves the reason for the Flood, any specific description of the sin, rather poorly developed, compared with the other texts; but perhaps that was felt to be unnecessary since the Flood was so well known that it did not seem to require an extensive rationale. By means of a significant re-writing of the traditional flood story J was able to continue his main themes: the inevitability of human sin (6:5-7; 8:21), the necessity of punishment (6:7), salvation in the midst of judgment (6:8; 8:21-22; and all that is said about the ark: cf. 7:23b), and the suffering of the cosmos for human sin (6:7; 7:4, 22-23; 8:21-22). We have also found some additions to J's major themes: Yahweh's inner struggle (6:6-7; 8:21-22) and the intention to start over with a faithful remnant (6:8; 7:1, 23).

The Flood seems to fit P's concerns somewhat more neatly, for it can be told so as to correspond with P's views of humanity, the world, and evil expressed in ch. 1. Evil, which was banished to the fringes of God's orderly cosmos in 1:2, has loosed its bonds and corrupted the whole earth in 6:11-13. The Flood represents the undoing of creation, but not as a victory of evil over God's will for order. Rather, God permits the chaos of flood waters to destroy the corrupted creation so that he may start over (6:13, 17, 18-21; 7:21; 8:1). Universal judgment fits P's theology of evil more neatly than J's. Noah as a righteous man fits better also, because of P's emphasis on humanity as appointed to rule over the world. Hence it is not surprising that P uses the word "covenant" apparently prematurely in 6:18, for in 9:1-17 the rainbow covenant will restore humanity to its appropriate place of superiority in the new world. That covenant also picks up J's theme of grace, for it requires nothing from its recipients; but it takes P's special form in that it is a covenant with all that lives, continuing the cosmic emphasis.

The special emphases that appear in P's version of the Flood also fit the suggested exilic setting of that work. P puts less emphasis on perennial human sinfulness, and more on the evil that corrupts the whole world and produces a deluge comparable in its destructive power to the recent experiences of the exiles. P also places a strong emphasis, much needed in the exilic community, on God's continuing assurance of blessing for the remnant.

Despite certain differences J and P fit together very well because they both preserve the basic integrity of the traditional flood story and because their differences in theology complement one another. J's stress on human rebellion is a necessary corrective to a possible misunderstanding of P, from whom one might conclude that evil is primarily external. But there is no real contrast between the sources. In both the whole world suffers. Neither wants to glorify Noah overmuch by developing stories of his saintly behavior, as interpreters have done ever since. Both deal with the difficult concept of God deciding to cleanse and purge by means of wholesale destruction and introduce the possibility that God may start over in a radical way. We have seen from J's conclusion (8:21) that the Flood leaves us with no answer as to whether such a procedure does any good, except for the negative comment that the Flood did not change human nature and the assurance that this is not the way God will continue to work in history.

The theme of purging and cleansing does reappear in Scripture, however. The story of the complete destruction of Sodom and Gomorrah except for one righteous man and his family (Gen. 19) is a close parallel to the Flood, only on a smaller scale; but salvation did not come from the loins of Lot. In the wilderness materials, God several times threatens to wipe out rebellious Israel and start over with one righteous man, Moses; but each time Moses himself persuades God to persevere (Exod. 32:7-14; Num. 14:11-19). Ezekiel interpreted Israel's early history as including three such threats by God, each of which was overruled by God's own faithfulness to his nature (Ezek. 20:8-9, 13-17, 21-22). But the preexilic prophets, Ezekiel included, did reach the conclusion that the end of the monarchy and the experience of exile represented God's deliberate intention to start all over (cf. Jer. 18:1-11). As the OT understands the exile, this radical act, unlike the Flood, did produce a radical change in those who survived (Jer. 31:31-34; Ezek. 36:25-27; 37:1-14). Perhaps this is why later apocalyptic literature can use the concept of the destruction and recreation of the cosmos, which originated with the Flood story, with more hope for a positive result than could have been drawn from reading Gen. 8:21-22. And we may wonder whether the theme of cleansing and purging by destroying does not also appear in the Crucifixion.

101

RESTORATION
AFTER THE FLOOD

Genesis 9:1-17

This section is P's conclusion to the Flood story. It corresponds in a limited way with J's conclusion, as a comparison of Gen. 9:1-7 with 8:22 and 9:8-17 with 8:21 shows. But since it introduces several subjects of intrinsic interest apart from the Flood, it will be treated in a separate section here. These verses contain no narrative; rather, they take the form of two speeches of God to Noah.

Renewal of the Blessing at Creation (9:1-7)

The most striking feature of 9:1-7 is the many references to Gen. 1. As the earth now lies a wasteland, God reestablishes the order of creation, with special emphasis on the prominence of the human, including one new privilege. The blessing of 1:28 is repeated in 9:1. God's intention is to restore the earth to its former abundance of life. The Flood was an episode, not a full end (despite 6:13). Human rule over all other creatures, first established in 1:28 with the verbs *kabash* ("subdue") and *radah* ("have dominion") is reaffirmed, but with stronger words. Humans will be the fear and terror of every living thing (9:2). The restoration is not a return to paradise, as vv. 3-6 make even clearer. This post-Flood world is the world we know, filled with violence and fear.

In v. 3 a new privilege is granted to humans, the right to kill animals so as to eat meat. So Israel's practice of eating meat is associated with a divine permission, granted to all human beings in the primordial period. Note that the wording here refers back to 1:29. The special dietary restrictions placed on Israel at Mt. Sinai are not alluded to here; human beings in general are allowed to eat any kind of meat.

As J recorded in 2:16-17 God's gift of food with one restriction attached, so P adds a restriction to the gift of the right to eat meat. Meat may not be eaten with "its life," defined here and elsewhere as its blood (cf. Lev. 17:11, 14; Deut. 12:23). We today see two focuses in Gen. 9:3-6, eating blood in vv. 3-4 and shedding the blood of humans in vv. 5-6; but for the Hebrews the two were closely related. Since they understood the blood to be the life essence of a creature, the restrictions they placed on the shedding and use of blood were continual reminders to them of the conviction that all life belongs to God and under no circumstances may be treated in a random or arbitrary way by human beings. Killing animals for food was permitted; but in early times probably all slaughter was sacrificial, and the blood had to be poured out to God (cf. Lev. 1:5; 7:26-27; 17:10-14; 1 Sam. 14:31-38). Later, when meat could be prepared for food without sacrifice, the blood still had to be treated in a special way (Deut. 12:23-24). There is no evidence that they thought the blood was sacred or contained some unique power (note that in Deuteronomy it is to be poured out "like water"); the only reason ever given for this commandment about the blood is that it is the life of the animal. Only God can give life, and so every life that is taken involves responsibility to God for having done so.

The connection between killing animals for food and taking human life thus becomes clear. But God allows for *no* taking of human life. The verb translated "require a reckoning" in the RSV (Gen. 9:5; NEB "demand satisfaction") makes God the enforcer of the prohibition, but as in other passages (Deut. 18:19; Ezek. 33:6) specifically what "satisfaction" or how he will obtain it is not indicated. Earlier in Genesis, Cain was not executed, but exiled as a result of committing murder. The only answer we are given comes in Gen. 9:6, but there are questions about how it should be interpreted. Is it a legal form, thus ordering capital punishment? Or is it a proverbial form, only describing present conditions in human society without approving or disapproving? It seems closest in form to legal sentences such as Exod. 21:12, 15-17; 22:19-20, although proverbs may have a similar form (cf. Prov. 21:13). Martin Luther took this verse to be the source of all civil law, granting humans power over life and death, hence over everything else. The OT will eventually order the taking of life by other humans, in commands to execute the death penalty for crimes destructive of human society and in commands to wage war under certain circumstances, but behind all that remains this valuation of every human life that reveals those commands to be accommodations to the continuing sinfulness J speaks of in Gen. 8:21. As we consider the whole biblical message concerning war and capital punishment, this text should not be seen as an authorization so much as implying a challenge: Can't we do better? That is because the reason given for God's special valuation of human life is profound, indeed disturbing. It alludes to 1:27, "God created man in his own image." Commenting on 9:6, John

Calvin provides a good summation of the impact of that sentence: "No one can be injurious to his brother without wounding God himself."

This section concludes (v. 7) as it began, repeating part of 1:28, to emphasize that the will of God is fruitfulness and life, not death.

The Covenant with Noah (9:8-17)

This is the first of four covenants recorded in the OT. The others are with Abraham (J, Gen. 15; P, Gen. 17), with Israel at Sinai (Exod. 19–34), and with David (2 Sam. 7; cf. Pss. 89, 132). As with any agreement, three elements are essential to the definition of a covenant: (1) the parties involved; (2) the contents of the agreement; (3) the means of maintenance. Since this passage is very repetitious, it will be economical to discuss the three elements rather than to follow it verse by verse.

All commentators remark about the wordiness of these verses. Some take this as evidence of two recensions, but not enough difference can be demonstrated in what is said from verse to verse to isolate two versions of the same speech. Others attribute the repetition to the Priestly style, and that seems more likely. As it now stands, almost half the words in the section refer to the recipients of the covenant, leaving no doubt about where the emphasis presently lies.

(1) The parties involved. In this case there is no hint of a mutual agreement, but we do find a giver and a recipient. On one side stands God, the giver, and on the other the recipients, everyone else. Here P uses the verb *heqim* ("establish"); but elsewhere he uses *ntn* ("give"), which is highly appropriate, for this covenant features no reciprocity of any kind: God is the actor and all others the beneficiaries. Noah and his sons can be addressed as representatives of the human race; but this is not merely a "covenant with Noah," for included are "every living creature that is with you, the birds, the cattle, and every beast of the earth with you" (Gen. 9:10; cf. vv. 12, 13, 15, 16, 17, where the recipients are named in a variety of ways). Furthermore, all generations of the living creatures of earth are included. This is the only covenant that involves more than human beings on earth; as such it is a fitting continuation of P's universal outlook, which we have seen in chs. 1 and 6–8.

(2) Content. The message given briefly by J in 8:21-22 is emphatically stated here by P. The Flood is not to be understood as a paradigm of God's dealings with the earth, for his way is one of patience and forbearance. Indeed, sin must be dealt with and evil must be vanquished, but God intends to find another way than

wiping out and starting over. The content of this covenant is a rein-
forcement of the promise in 9:1-7, that God's intention for the earth
is life, not death.

Disaster still threatens, chaos seems about to break in upon us at
times, life does fall apart for some, and we experience anew the impact of the Flood. But the covenant with Noah is God's assurance
that such unexplainable disasters—the tornados, earthquakes, vol-
canic eruptions; the cancer and birth defects—are not punishments
sent by him for someone's sins, but are part of the remaining challenge to his rule of order, which he fights against.

(3) Maintenance of the covenant. If the animals are among the recipients of this promise, what can they do in response? Answer:
Nothing. Neither can Noah and his descendants do anything to in-
sure that the covenant remains in force. This is the most striking example of what has been called the covenant of divine commitment.
It is very different from the covenant made with Israel at Mt. Sinai,
for that required obedience from the people (Exod. 19:5-8; 24:3;
34:10-28). The Sinai covenant has been called one of human obliga-
tion. The covenant with Noah is more like those with Abraham and
David, in that in none of them do we find any indication that a
human being could do anything that could nullify it. God maintains
each of these covenants by his own faithfulness; but the covenant
with Noah is the most extreme, for Abraham and his descendants,
David and his descendants could respond to God's promise, whereas
a response from the animals is neither necessary nor possible.

God's choice of the rainbow as the sign of this covenant (unlike
circumcision, Gen. 17; or the law, Exod. 20–23) is appropriate, for
it is something human beings can do nothing about. It has a natural
connection with the contents of the covenant; for as the rainbow is
a sign of the end of a storm, it now is intended to be a reminder (to
God! Gen. 9:15) that there will be no more world-destroying floods.
Since the time of Julius Wellhausen, most commentators have interpreted this "bow" as a hint that God has put away his weapon (cf.
Ps. 7:12-13; Lam. 2:4; 3:12; Hab. 3:9-11); but since the Primeval
history makes no other use of the tradition of Yahweh the warrior, it
seems more likely that only the rainbow is denoted here, as several
recent interpreters have concluded.

This is to be an "eternal covenant," dependent for its maintenance
solely on the faithfulness of God. Although no response is required
from human beings, certainly we can see one that is appropriate—
and necessary, if the covenant is to mean anything to us—and that is
trust. The prophet of the exile whom we call Second Isaiah recog-

nized that divine faithfulness and human trust were the essence of the covenant with Noah when he applied it to the exilic experience in Isa. 54:9-10. Second Isaiah appropriately used the term *hesed* ("steadfast love"), and called God's faithfulness in preserving us from existence in a mindless, meaningless cosmos, hurtling to certain destruction or slowly dying like an untended fire, his "covenant of peace."

In rabbinic tradition this text took on great importance as a key to the relationship between Yahweh, who had chosen Israel as his special people, and the other peoples of the world. Since all human beings are descended from Noah, the Gentiles are obviously included in the covenant of Gen. 9, but the rabbis did not quite understand it as a covenant without stipulations. As they developed the concept of the Noahic covenant, they concluded that Adam had been given six commandments: (1) institute civil courts; (2) refrain from idolatry, (3) . . . blasphemy, (4) . . . shedding of blood, (5) . . . unchastity, and (6) . . . seizing what belongs to another. A seventh, which prohibited cutting a limb from a living animal, was added in the time of Noah. It was taught that Gentiles who observed these commandments had done all God expected from them, and so a place for a direct relationship between their God and the Gentiles was provided in Jewish teaching. Some echoes of the Noahic covenant can be found in the letter that the leaders of the church in Jerusalem sent to Gentile converts to Christianity, recorded in Acts 15:23-29.

HAM'S SIN
AND THE CURSE OF CANAAN

Genesis 9:18-29

Repopulating the earth after the Flood became the responsibility of Noah's sons, Shem, Ham, and Japheth, as Gen. 10 will show; and it is that important function, their only function in the Primeval history, that explains the references to them that have appeared earlier (5:32; 6:10; 7:13). But before the families of the earth are listed a strange incident is recorded, involving Noah, his three sons, and apparently one grandson. It is brief and full of non sequiturs that have left every scholar baffled, and parts of the account cannot be explained. More attention will be paid to the competing scholarly theories here than is customary for this Commentary because of the appalling misuse of this passage to justify the enslaving of Africans, the descendants of Ham.

This short passage is composed of four types of material: genealogical information (9:18-19, 28-29), a bit of the history of culture (v. 20), a story about a family problem (vv. 22-24), and a curse and blessing (vv. 25-27). There is no reason why these four types could not fit together nicely, but in this case they do not. The glaring problem is Noah's cursing of Canaan for something that his father Ham had done. Various attempts to explain this will be discussed in connection with the relevant verses. The combination of materials also raises a question about the major intention of the passage. Is it principally an archetypal story about family relationships, like Gen. 4, or does it intend to explain relationships among ethnic groups, like Gen. 21 and 27? Since the movement from seeing one's father's nakedness to the curse of slavery does not seem to involve any natural cause-effect relationship, it seems most likely that an early story about the disruption of normal family relationships, in which Ham was probably the subject throughout, was later modified by the introduction of Canaan so as to become a vehicle to express Israel's negative opinion of Canaanite culture.

In the previous section it was noted that the Flood is not presented as a solution to the human dilemma; rather, the covenant with Noah implies that God intends to find another way, although no hint of what that way will be is yet provided. In J's account of the primeval period two more stories (9:20-27; 11:1-9) are included in order to show that the Flood was not followed by a time of perfection, but that human beings and society at large remained "only evil continually." In a few verses, immediately after God's reassurances to Noah (8:21-22 in J, 9:1-17 in the present context), three of the perennial evils afflicting humanity are introduced: drunkenness, disrespect for parents, and slavery. J offers comment only on the second of them.

Ham's Sin (9:20-24)

The genealogical note in vv. 18-19 connects this passage with the genealogy of ch. 5 and looks ahead to ch. 10 with its comment, "from these the whole earth was peopled." The name of Canaan as Ham's son is added, without apparent reason at this point, but it is present in order to prepare us for the passage that follows.

A note on the development of culture appears in 9:20, with Noah apparently being given credit for planting the first vineyard. Grapes were an important part of Israel's economy during its life in the land of Canaan, so that one of the great pilgrimage feasts, Succoth, occurred in conjunction with the grape harvest in the fall (Deut. 16:13-15). The OT frequently refers to the blessings of the vine, and it became a symbol for fertility, refreshment, and abundant life (Ps. 80:8-16; Isa. 5:1-7; 27:2-6; Ezek. 19:10-14). The negative effects of wine on the senses were not overlooked, as Lev. 10:9; Prov. 23:31-35; 31:6-7 indicate. Noah's drunkenness is not the subject of this story, however, but his uncontrolled behavior simply provides the unfortunate setting for the event that occurs. He is lying naked in his tent, having passed out, as Gen. 9:24 reveals. The danger of losing one's clothes in an inebriated state is commented on in Lam. 4:21; Hab. 2:15 as well, and the general feeling of shame at being seen naked is frequently mentioned in the OT (Exod. 20:26; 2 Sam. 6:20; 10:4-5; Isa. 47:3; Ezek. 16:37). Respect for the person, in Israel, always involved the covering of the sexual parts, so that to see someone naked was one of the most extreme ways possible to dishonor that person. It is necessary to understand this point of view in order to make sense of what happens next.

Ham apparently entered his father's tent for some reason and saw his father lying there asleep and naked. He reported it to his two brothers, who then took very careful precautions to see to it that Noah was covered without looking at him themselves (Gen. 9:23). This action is the only thing recorded in any detail in the entire story.

Commentators, ancient and modern, have offered extensive discussion concerning what Ham's sin really was. Many have attributed to him some gross sexual sin such as castration, sodomy, or incest (intercourse with Noah's wife). Explicit stories about such interfamily tensions leading to those very acts, in the myths and legends of the ancient Near East, have been cited as parallels, and Ham's "real sin" has been deduced from the parallels rather than from what the story in its present form actually says. But the OT elsewhere does not shrink from telling such stories in plain words, as Gen. 18 (Lot and his guests in Sodom), Gen. 19 (Lot and his daughters), Gen. 38 (Tamar and Judah), 2 Sam. 13 (Amnon and his half-sister Tamar), and other passages clearly show.

Here it is explicitly said that Noah uncovered himself, and the fact that the only thing Ham did was to see him in a naked state is confirmed by the actions of Shem and Japheth to correct the problem. Hence it seems that Claus Westermann is correct in reviving a traditional explanation, tame as it may seem in comparison with the others, recognizing that the issue is one of respect for parents. The earliest form of this story probably added one more typical family problem to those that J had already presented (dissension between husband and wife in ch. 3; dissension between siblings in ch. 4): dissension between parent and child. The story certainly contains an aura of the sexual tensions that may afflict the interrelationships of family members, but the issue presented here is probably not narrowly sexual in its implications. In a culture such as that of ancient Israel, where the parent was teacher, judge, and priest, the disrespect of a child was virtually equivalent to the crime of treason today, as the provision for the death penalty in Deut. 21:18-21 reveals. Given Israel's association of nakedness with extreme disrespect and its awareness that the breakdown of the parent-child relationship was tantamount to the breakdown of social order, it is easy to understand that a most serious issue has arisen here. But this time God does not intervene, as in Gen. 3 and 4; it is Noah who takes action, and the curse he utters is directed toward Ham's son, Canaan, rather than Ham himself! Furthermore, the one cursed is called his youngest son (9:24), whereas Ham is the middle son and Canaan the grandson. This remains the unsolved problem of this passage and is the source of the worst misinterpretation of it.

Noah Curses Canaan (9:25-27)

The defenders of slavery in 19th-cent. America ignored the unexplained transition from Ham to Canaan in Noah's curse and drew the simplistic conclusion that since (according to ch. 10) Ham was the ancestor of some African groups, then his black descendants may rightfully be enslaved. They ignored or explained away the plain fact that the curse is directed against Canaan and that Canaan was neither black nor African. Other interpretations of the passage include some that are more fanciful, but none with such appalling ethical consequences. The midrashim said Noah intended to beget a fourth son to be his slave but that Ham castrated him in order to prevent that, so Ham's fourth son was cursed with slavery. A recent interpretation claims Ham witnessed intercourse between Noah and his wife and by so doing obtained power over Noah, who then could not curse Ham; Noah therefore cursed Canaan to prevent Ham from passing on this power. Yet another sexual interpretation says that Ham committed incest with his mother and Canaan was the product, so was cursed with slavery. Less imaginative is the assumption that for the curse to be fair, Canaan must have shared somehow in the guilt of his father. Each such approach rewrites the story in order to tell us what really happened.

Slightly different explanations attempt to reconstruct the history of tradition. One approach concludes that Ham and Canaan were originally identified as the same person, so that there was no discontinuity between the guilty act and the curse. Later this identity was forgotten and the explanation "Ham, the father of Canaan" was inserted. Another suggests there were two traditions about Noah's sons, the variant one calling them Shem, Japheth, and Canaan. Canaan, the youngest (9:24), originally committed the sin; then when this story was accommodated to the dominant tradition (Shem, Ham, Japheth), confusion was introduced.

The explanation I prefer is based on the identification of two uses for the story, the original an account of recurring family tensions and the modification of it an expression of ethnic hatreds. The story of disrespect for one's parent was originally told of Ham, concluding with a curse directed against him. Ham may have been the natural subject for the story because he is the only one of the three sons identified with a specific nation in the OT, namely Egypt (Ps. 78:51; 105:23, 27; 106:22). Nudity was commonplace in Egyptian styles of dress, and the Israelite memory of Egypt was dominated by their own experience of slavery there. In the traditional genealogies Ham and Canaan were associated (Gen. 10:6); so at some later time, when feelings about Canaanites were far more powerful than the memories of Egypt, Canaan's name may have been introduced into 9:18, 22, and the curse directed toward him. Why either Ham or

Canaan should be called "youngest" (or "smallest," another possible translation; v. 24) still remains without an adequate explanation.

Extensive efforts have been made to explain the ethnic dimension of the story in order to account for the blessing of Shem's God and the peaceful relationships between Shem and Japheth. But so far no attempt to locate a period in Israel's history where this would fit what is known of international relationships has proved to be fully convincing.

Does the story have any value? Martin Luther was blunt, calling it "indeed a silly and altogether unprofitable little story." A modern commentator, J. C. L. Gibson, has been just as negative, writing, "The distasteful story of the curse on Canaan ought not to be in the Bible." Surely its expression of hatred for the Canaanites and its justification of slavery are of no value to anyone. However, in the light of Israel's growing recognition of slavery as a problem (compare Exod. 21:1-11 with Deut. 15:12-18 and Lev. 25:39-46), with the appearance of "your brother" in the restrictions that Deuteronomy and Leviticus put on slavery, and the accusation of Amos that Tyre's slave trade violated the "covenant of brotherhood" (Amos 1:9), this story may fit as an early stage in a developing acknowledgment that slavery is a radical denial of brotherhood, the result of a violation of basic family relationships.

If the essence of the story is the insistence that respect of children for their parents is absolutely essential for a stable society to endure, the question remains whether such a concern can be taken seriously anymore, when in our time such family solidarity is either breaking down or has already virtually been demolished. That is not a question one author can answer. The answer may vary depending on the culture, and it will certainly vary depending on one's individual outlook. In our time, what is perhaps most discouraging about even contemplating Israel's insistence and the difference between the foundations of their culture and of many modern cultures is this: If they were right, is there anything at all that we can do about it now?

THE TABLE OF NATIONS
Genesis 10:1-32

This chapter represents a unique piece of intellectual activity in the ancient world, for it is an effort to classify all the known peoples of the earth by their lands, languages, families, and nations (10:5, 20, 31). It presents an "ecumenical" outlook of its own kind; for despite its acknowledgment of the elements just mentioned that distinguish peoples from one another, it emphasizes the existence of a unity binding all humanity together. All are children of one father, Noah, so there can be no differences in kind to separate us (9:19; 10:32).

Seventy (or seventy-one, depending on how one counts) "nations" are listed in the chapter. Some, such as Egypt and Canaan, are well known to us; others, such as Riphath and Anamim, are completely unknown. Quite likely such extensive knowledge of the peoples of the ancient world was the result of commercial activity that brought to Israel the products of regions far away, and with them the names and fragments of information about groups the Israelites had never seen. It is significant that many of the same names occur in Ezek. 27, the allegory of the Phoenician trading ship; and the nations that we can identify seem to fit best the period of the 7th and early 6th centuries. Note that Persia is not mentioned, and that country would scarcely have been omitted after the middle of the 6th century.

The principles of classification given in Gen. 10:5, 20, 31 can be expressed in our terminology as geographic, linguistic, ethnic, and political; but so far every effort by scholars to make the divisions fit those criteria has failed. It is not a strict linguistic division, since the Canaanites (said to be Hamites) spoke a Semitic language, and the Elamite language was not Semitic (although they are said to be Shemites). The geographic principle works well for Japheth, since all those groups seem to have lived to the far north of Israel, but creates great problems for understanding Ham. Cush is normally identified with Ethiopia, but the sons listed in v. 7 are Arabian tribes; and worse yet, another son, Nimrod, is associated entirely with Mesopotamian cities. The political principle is preferred by most commentators, since it would explain the association of Canaan with Egypt. For long periods of time, Canaan was within the sphere of political and commercial influence of the Egyptians. A sociocultural explanation of the division has also been offered, suggesting that this chapter is similar to Gen. 4:20-22, which speaks of the ancestors of herdsmen, musicians, and metalworkers. It is proposed that the descendants of Shem are all nomadic groups; those of Ham, groups enjoying settled, city culture; and those of Japheth, seafarers. As with every other principle, this one also does not account for every member of each group. A source critical analysis does not solve the problem, either. The structure of P's contribution becomes clear and simple once J is removed (10:1b, 8-19, 21, 24-30 are assigned to J); but the problems mentioned above still remain. We still can do little more than admit we do not understand the reasons for including some of the nations where they are.

One of the most interesting parts of the chapter deals with Nimrod, who is introduced as the first empire builder. The account seems out of place to us, for he is called a son of Ham and yet is associated with the great cities of Mesopotamia, which were all occupied by Semitic peoples during the biblical period. This is another of J's notes concerning the development of human culture. It is historically accurate, in that civilization as we know it—the development of city-states—began in southern Mesopotamia (represented here by Babel, Erech, and Accad) and later extended northward into Assyria (vv. 11-12). This note is neutral in tone, like 4:17-22 and 9:20. It does not follow the pattern of the stories of Cain and Abel or the tower of Babel, which express negative judgments about what has gone wrong in human culture. This is somewhat remarkable in that the list of cities includes Israel's deadly enemies, Babel and Nineveh. In postbiblical traditions, Nimrod was made the builder of the tower of Babel and his might (10:8) was presented as arrogance.

Chapters 10 and 11 are associated in several ways. The theme of the concentration of political power that is central to 11:1-9 is anticipated in 10:8-12, and the dispersion of people throughout the earth that concludes 11:1-9 is already described in detail in ch. 10. Indeed, the two passages may seem to be out of order, since 11:1 tells us all people spoke one language, whereas ch. 10 uses language as one of its principles of division; but there may be a theological reason for the present order. The nations in ch. 10, in their diversity and distribution throughout the earth, do not yet stand under the judgment of 11:1-9, so that a remarkably neutral attitude toward those enemies and rivals of Israel is presented.

This ecumenical outlook is more significant to us than the principles of classification that may have been used. As an intellectual achievement the Table of Nations still puzzles us, but as a reflection of Israel's theology it is a quite remarkable statement. Note that Israel is nowhere mentioned, not even in anticipation. Chapter 10 ends with the descendants of Shem, because it is his genealogy that will be resumed in 11:10; but the chapter stands as a complete unit in its own right, as the introduction and conclusion show (10:1, 32). Without referring to ch. 11 one would not have a clue as to where Israel will belong in the Table of Nations. Here we find expressed an interest in all people, in their own right. The chapter is thus a significant anticipation of 12:3, "by you all the families of the earth shall bless themselves." Given the very natural and understandable hatred expressed for the Canaanites in Deuteronomy, for Nineveh in Nahum, and for Babylon in Isa. 47, it is quite remarkable that elsewhere in the OT an openness even to those traditional enemies is expressed. Here and there we find evidence that Israel could believe that the pagan nations had a certain relationship to Yahweh in their own right (cf. Gen. 16, 36; Amos 1–2). And in eschatological passages, the outlook that is only implicit in Gen. 10 is made explicit, in hopes for the day to come when even the old enemies will live together in peace (cf. Isa. 2:2-4; 19:18-25; Ezek. 29:13-16). When Paul said to the Athenians, "And he made from one every nation of men to live on all the face of the earth, having determined allotted periods and the boundaries of their habitation, that they should seek God, in the hope that they might feel after him and find him" (Acts 17:26-27), he was not expressing a peculiarly NT idea, but was reaffirming a hope implicit in Gen. 10 and which became explicit in Israel's eschatology.

THE CITY OF BABEL
Genesis 11:1-9

The story seems out of place at first reading, since it explains how people came to be dispersed throughout the earth just after ch. 10 has presented in detail the results of God's plan for repopulation after the Flood (cf. 10:32). Source analysis makes the problem somewhat less severe, for ch. 10 is basically P's version of replenishing the earth, while 11:1-9 is J's rather different explanation. This still leaves the question why the final editor did not consider 11:1-9 to be an appropriate introduction to ch. 10, especially since Shem's genealogy in 10:21-31 would then have been followed very naturally by Abraham's family tree in 11:10-32. The choice to put the Babel story just here must have been deliberate. If we notice that the continuing story of Abraham does not begin in ch. 12 but in 11:10, then Babel is the end of the Primeval history, the last event recorded before salvation history begins. As we examine the story, then, we should consider what makes it an appropriate conclusion to Gen. 1–11, this prologue to the story of God's saving work.

The story contains a single reference to a tower with its top in the heavens (11:4), and this brief phrase has caught and held the imaginations of writers and artists through the ages. Fantastic legends have been produced to embroider the story, making it an arrogant attempt to storm heaven itself, while painters have tended to represent the building of the tower in a peaceful way, as a great marvel of human cooperation. The tower of Babel, including many of the legendary embellishments, has become a part of every culture that knows the OT. Its symbolism will no doubt continue to be effective, even though a careful rereading of the passage suggests that the real emphasis is not on the tower at all. Note that the people begin to build a city and a tower (v. 4), which Yahweh comes down to see (v. 5). But the end of the story does not find it necessary to mention the tower at all, saying only that they left off building the city (v. 8). In order to point out where the emphasis does *not* lie, I have called this section "The City of Babel" rather than "The Tower of Babel."

This story forms the culmination of J's sequence dealing with alienation: husband from wife (ch. 3), brother from brother (ch. 4), children from parents (ch. 9), and now, peoples from other peoples. In each of these accounts, alienation at the human level is accompanied by—indeed, caused by—alienation of humans from their God (most clearly expressed in chs. 3 and 4). In 11:1-9 the limits of the family are transcended and we do not read of individuals, but of the "sons of *adam*" (v. 5); at the end of the story they have populated the whole earth in separate language groups. This is the final piece of information about the condition of ourselves and the world we live in that needs to be provided before the story of Abraham begins. That story will begin to focus on one family among the nations of the earth; but it is a family for and with whom God will begin to counter with blessing the alienation that curses all the families of the earth (12:2-3).

The Builders (11:1-4)

The story begins and ends with the issue of the different languages that divide us from one another by making communication difficult. The idea that a common language was once spoken by all people is probably the result of moving from one's own, homogeneous group into contact with others whom one cannot understand. It seems wrong, somehow; they are human like us, and so the inability to communicate can be extremely frustrating. I can remember the puzzlement of my children when they began to play with some Swiss children in a Geneva park and discovered that, although they were speaking words to one another, the words did not mean anything. Such experiences have led to efforts to account for the existence of different languages. Many popular theories assume that all present languages have developed from one original tongue—usually one's own. For example, one scholar attempted to prove that God spoke to Adam in Norwegian and Adam answered him in Danish. Since the OT is in Hebrew, however, earlier linguists tended to assume that was the original language. One experiment was proposed that would have taken a newborn child to a deserted island, in the care of a nurse who was mute, in order to find out what language the child would speak when it grew up. We are sure now that the child would not have spoken any language, let alone classical Hebrew, but fortunately the experiment was not carried out. Modern linguistic scholars find it impossible to derive all languages on earth from any single prototype.

The introduction (11:1), with its emphasis on oneness (the word translated "few" in the RSV is a form of the word "one"), alerts us to expect a story that will move from unity to diversity. But surely diversity in itself is not wrong. P's Creation story revels in the variety of "kinds" that God made and pronounced good. So the question that follows us through the story is, What is going wrong here? Several answers have been offered.

No specific group is mentioned in v. 2; the RSV supplies "men" as a subject where the Hebrew simply says "they." It is as if the "whole earth" of v. 1 did the migrating. The verb is used of the movements of groups such as Abraham's caravan in 12:5-9. The direction of their movement is not perfectly clear, since Hebrew is not as explicit in directions as we would like. It may be "eastward" or "from the east"; but their destination, Shinar, is not uncertain, for it is known to be Mesopotamia (cf. 10:10; Dan. 1:2). The verse provides a brief description of the change from a migrant group to a settled people.

Mesopotamia is a place where no stone is available for building; but at the very beginnings of culture there, human inventiveness found a way to build permanent structures by molding bricks that were then baked either in the sun or in ovens. The reference to the development of brick-making in Gen. 11:3 is presented from the point of view of an author in the central part of Canaan, where stone was plentiful and mud was used for mortar. (Massive brick structures may also be found in the Philistine cities of the coastal plain, where stone is not so readily available.) The author had accurate information about Mesopotamian building techniques, since bitumen was used there as mortar and it was not common elsewhere.

At last in v. 4 we are given a reason for the activity that has been described. They intend to build a city and a great tower. This is not presented as a novelty, as the first city, since Cain had already been called a city builder (4:17). And nothing in the story indicates that it represents a thoroughgoing antiurban point of view, as some scholars have claimed. The tower, about which so much has been written, may reflect a knowledge of the gigantic Mesopotamian temple towers, called ziggurats; but so little is said of it in the story that those interpretations that call the passage an attack on pagan religion, or make it a story of an attempted ascent into heaven, go far beyond the text and overlook its own emphases. This is a case where the discoveries of archaeology, which enable us to visualize the ziggurat and to understand its meaning and use, may have misled rather than helped us. It seems likely that the expression "with its top in the heavens" is not to be taken any more literally than "the cities are great and fortified up to heaven" in Deut. 1:28; 9:1. The words of the story itself make the tower nothing more than the most prominent feature of a great city.

Two motives for this massive building project are now cited: "let us make a name for ourselves" and "lest we be scattered abroad upon the face of the whole earth." This reference to "name" stands in significant contrast to a promise that appears very near to it. In Gen. 12:2 God says to Abram, "And I will bless you, and make your name great." "Name" in Hebrew denotes one's character and reputation, so Ezekiel says that God will act to restore Israel "for the sake of my holy name, which you have profaned among the nations" (Ezek. 36:22). Human beings may make a name for themselves without being condemned for undue pride or ambition (David, 2 Sam. 7:23), and this story makes no direct judgment of this motive of the city builders. The question remains, then, how much we should make of the context, the difference between God's promise to make a name for Abraham and the people's effort here to make a name for themselves. We may also wonder whether such an expression may be intended to recall the motive for the sin in Gen. 3, but the allusion is only a faint one.

The second motive has been accurately described as "anxiety." Being scattered abroad upon the face of the earth is obviously seen as a threat, leading to weakness and the inability to have all the good things that the concentration of their power and resources in a city can provide. When this concern is linked with God's reasoning in 11:6, we come nearer to an answer to the question, What is going wrong here?

Intervention/Prevention (11:5-9)

The story is clearly divided into two halves, with v. 5 the turning point. In vv. 2-4 human action and speech are recorded; in vv. 6-8 God is the actor and speaker; and v. 5 is the "hinge" connecting the two parts, with reference first to God, then to the "sons of men." Most commentators have remarked that the rather strange expression, for an Israelite writer, "And the LORD came down to see . . . ," must be taken as ironic. Certainly this is not the only place where God is depicted in rather human terms as conducting an investigation (cf. 18:20-21); but in this context, where people are building a "skyscraper," one can scarcely help but think the writer got some enjoyment from depicting God as having to get closer just to see that project which was so gigantic from a human perspective.

God's judgment of the situation (11:6) does perhaps give more credit to the builders than the author of the story is inclined to do. He repeats the words of the introduction to the story, concerning the unity of this people, and draws from them a conclusion that seems disturbing to him. This immediately raises the question for us as to what is wrong with unity. The only answer provided by the story is in the last part of this verse, and it must be the key to the whole passage: "and this is only the beginning of what they will do; and nothing that they propose to do will now be impossible for them." A superficial reading of this may conclude that God sees in human prowess a real threat to himself, and so proposes to act in self-defense. If this were a story from Mesopotamian or Greek religion, such a reading might be fully appropriate; but it violates everything said about God in the rest of the Bible. As we set this statement in the context provided by the rest of J's work in Gen. 1-11, a better reading appears. This statement fits the theme of a fallen human being that has been consistently presented in the stories recorded by J. It acknowledges that human beings have fantastic powers, and have in many respects become like God (3:22). They can do marvelous things, of which the city and tower are examples; but unfortunately they are unable to use the powers given to them without bringing pain into the world. They are neither wise enough nor good enough to be their own gods. God's prediction, "nothing that they propose to do will now be impossible for them," does not—in J's thinking—represent a threat to God, but a threat to humanity. The more power they are able to concentrate, the more harm they will be able to do to themselves and the world. So we ought to understand God's decision (11:7-8) as not so much the punishment of sin as a preventive act to avert a great potential evil (cf. the interpretation of 3:22-23 offered above).

I have been using the word "power" as a key to the understanding of the passage, even though that word does not occur in the text, for the emphasis on unity and on human accomplishment in terms of city building point in that direction. God's intervention recorded in 11:7-8 also indicates that the problem is the concentration of too much power for human beings to use without great harm, for he destroys their unity by confusing their language so that they scatter, divided into linguistic groups. Consequently, the city remains unfinished. In the ancient world the city was the first and the most obvious example of the human ability to concentrate talent and resources so as to multiply power—commercial, political, social, and religious power. But the story does not represent a thoroughgoing, antiurban point of view, for that would be out of harmony with the general outlook of the Bible as well. The city is recognized in Scripture as a great human accomplishment, where the best that we can produce may be found. Unfortunately those most awesome accumulations of power also result in the worst inflictions of pain, on our fellow human beings and on the world of nature. The underlying concern of this story, in keeping with the others in Gen. 1–11, is our need for protection from our own ability to use power to destroy rather than to bless.

Is this a sin and punishment story? No sin is ever explicitly identified, unlike the other stories we have dealt with. It seems better to call God's action here preventative or protective. Those who have interpreted Gen. 1–11 as the story of a crescendo of sin, climaxing in the tower of Babel, have probably read too much into 11:1-9. Instead, J's practice of concluding his stories of human misuse of God's blessings with a divine act involving a mixture of judgment and grace seems to appear here also. Human beings tried to do more than would be good for humanity in general. Accordingly, God intervened to thwart their immense project by confusing their speech, making life more difficult for them; but that also protected them from the worst that they could do to one another.

The scattering that the people feared became a reality because of their very efforts to avoid it. The concluding verses (vv. 8-9) speak of the scattering twice, because it sets the scene for the world in which Abraham will soon appear. An etymology for the name of the city Babylon is added, but only as an example of the kind of wordplay a Hebrew author enjoyed. The actual meaning of the name (Babilim, in its original spelling) is unknown, but the Babylonians had provided a popular etymology of their own, "the gate of the god." Now J provides a popular Hebrew etymology, comparing Babel with the verb *balal*, meaning "to confuse" or "mix." But this is not the point of the story, so having indulged in that bit of fun he repeats its proper conclusion in v. 9b. The scattering is ambiguous, just as God's action is a mixture of grace and judgment. The verb *(puts)* is one that Ezekiel uses frequently with regard to exile, an act of judgment with thoroughly negative connotations, but J uses the same verb in a neutral way in Gen. 10:18. In this story its use is judgmental, in that the scattering puts ambition in its proper place and is the result of the divisions caused by our different languages; yet it also provides for the repopulation of the whole earth after the Flood, which was God's intention. The Babel story recalls in several ways the major concerns of Gen. 3. It speaks of the mixture in human beings of godlikeness (making possible great achievements) with the sinful tendency that inevitably corrupts our every accomplishment. This is the theme that controls the way the story is told and accounts for the ambiguity of the scattering willed by God.

FROM THE PRIMEVAL ERA
TO THE HISTORY
OF SALVATION
Genesis 11:10-32

The Descendants of Shem (11:10-26)

This is the fourth list of names in the Primeval history (cf. chs. 4, 5, 10), but it marks a significant change in subject matter from those that preceded. The genealogies of chs. 4 and 5 represent the population of the earth, even though apparently the firstborn son of each individual is usually the only descendant listed. The Table of Nations explicitly intends to describe all the nations of the earth; it ends with one of the three sons of Noah, Shem, to whom five sons were born. But the new genealogy in 11:10-26 is concerned with only one of those sons, Arpachshad, so there now appears a narrowing down of attention, leading quickly to Terah and his three sons. Few details are given for the eight generations preceding Terah; only the age at the birth of the first son and the age at death, with the reference to the birth of other sons and daughters. No cultural notes or extra information about certain individuals appear, such as may be found in chs. 4, 5, and 10. The ages given gradually diminish to approach life spans known to us, as a way of saying that the primeval materials are now giving way to historical existence as we know it. Shem lived six hundred years and begot Arpachshad at age one hundred, but after that the ages of begetting (except for Terah) vary from twenty-nine to thirty-five, and the life spans drop first to the four hundreds, then the two hundreds.

Several of the names in this list appear as place names in northern Mesopotamia, around Haran (in Hebrew spelled differently from the name of Terah's son). Around 1000 B.C. this region was heavily populated with Aramean people who had migrated northward from the Arabian desert. It is the region in which Abraham's kinsman Laban lived (28:1-2). This genealogy is of significant historical interest, for it supplements the stories of Genesis involving relationships with the Aramean peoples around Haran (e.g., chs. 24, 28–31), and also helps to explain the beginning of the "historical credo" in Deut. 26:5: "A wandering Aramean was my father."

The Beginning of the History of Salvation (11:27-32)

The end of the Shem genealogy branches, as in Gen. 4 with Lamech's three sons and in ch. 5 with Noah's three. Only one of Terah's sons will be the recipient of God's promise, but the relationships between Abraham's family and those of his two brothers were important memories in Israel.

Haran was remembered as the father of Lot, about whom the traditions of the destruction of Sodom and Gomorrah circulated (Gen. 18–19). Lot was considered to be the ancestor of Moab and Ammon, so Israel acknowledged those neighboring nations—with whom relationships were often hostile—to be close relatives (cf. Deut. 23:3-6; Ruth 1:1-17; 4:13-22; 2 Sam. 8:2; Jer. 48:1-47; 49:1-6). Nahor and Milcah (Haran's daughter) were grandparents of Isaac's wife, Rebekah (Gen. 24:15), and her brother Laban (v. 29) was father of Jacob's wives, Leah and Rachel (29:1-20). Since Jacob was the father of the twelve tribes of Israel, this meant all Israel considered themselves to be descended on their mother's side from this branch of the family living in the territory of the Arameans around Haran. We cannot account for this tradition as easily as the stories about Lot, Moab, and Ammon, for the relationships between the historical Israel and that region do not seem to have been particularly close. But it must therefore be an accurate recollection of relationships with Aramean groups prior to the settlement of Israel in Canaan. This would account for the mention of Iscah (11:29), about whom nothing is known. She was probably included because of a vague memory that she represented a group with whom the ancestors of Israel were once related.

Terah migrated from Ur, far south in Mesopotamia, to Haran in the far north (v. 31). He is said to have been on his way to Canaan, but no reason is given for the journey. Knowing what we do about Abraham from ch. 12, the verse is tantalizing for its complete lack of theology, when it would seem there ought to be some. Legend has greatly expanded these few verses, creating a history of Abraham's early life (cf. the Apocalypse of Abraham), but all that seems to have been created much later than the material in Genesis. The expression "Ur of the Chaldees" is something of a problem, since the Chaldeans became politically dominant in south Mesopotamia only with the appearance of Nebuchadnezzar's father, Nabopolassar, late in the 7th century. It may be possible to associate the expression with an earlier period, however, since the Chaldeans were a branch of the Aramean migration that had settled in the marshlands around the mouths of the Tigris and Euphrates by ca. 1000. Terah's journey thus might be a reflection of the memory of those tribal movements, perhaps even recalling the settlement of the Chaldeans in the area around Ur. The migration with theological significance, however, as ch. 12 shows, is the one made by Abraham from Haran to Canaan.

This section's most important verse, theologically, states a negative—twice, in case we missed it the first time: "Now Sarai was barren; she had no child" (11:30). Twenty generations of genealogy have brought us to Abram, and it seems now that he is a person of no importance, for the story appears to end with him and Sarai. The author will not save the information about their childlessness in order to surprise us later. Indeed, it is the first piece of information he gives about them—and the only thing we know until Abram becomes the recipient of a promise. It is a promise addressed to emptiness.

> And I will make of you a great nation,
> and I will bless you, and make your name great,
>   so that you will be a blessing.
> I will bless those who bless you,
> and him who curses you I will curse;
> and by you all the families of the earth shall bless themselves.
>
> (Gen. 12:2-3)

The promise requires descendants, and it is addressed to Sarai as well as Abram, since only her son is a child of the promise (15:1-5; 21:9-13). "Now Sarai was barren; she had no child." The essence of the biblical message is contained in this non sequitur. Into God's good earth humans have succeeded in bringing suspicion of God's goodness; fear, envy, anger, oppression, and death. Now the result of twenty generations of replenishing the earth is a childless couple whom God proposes to make a blessing to all the nations of this disturbed and suffering earth. "The foolishness of God is wiser than men" (1 Cor. 1:25). Here in brief is the pattern of the way he finds to save us, choosing what is weak to confound the strong (Gen. 11:1-9), even bringing life out of death (8:17; Heb. 11:12), in order to show that he alone is sovereign and in order to demonstrate that another name for God's sovereignty is pure grace (Rom. 4:16-25; 1 Cor. 1:26-31; Phil. 2:5-11).

SELECTED BIBLIOGRAPHY

Commentaries

Blocher, Henri. *In the Beginning: The Opening Chapters of Genesis* (Downers Grove and Leicester: Inter-Varsity, 1984).

Brueggemann, Walter. *Genesis.* Interpretation (Atlanta: John Knox, 1982).

Calvin, John. *Commentaries on the First Book of Moses called Genesis,* vol. 1 (Grand Rapids: Wm. B. Eerdmans, 1948).

Cassuto, Umberto. *A Commentary on the Book of Genesis* (Jerusalem: Magnes and Oxford: Oxford University Press, 1961).

Coats, George W. *Genesis: With an Introduction to Narrative Literature.* The Forms of the Old Testament Literature 1 (Grand Rapids: Wm. B. Eerdmans, 1983).

Gibson, J. C. L. *Genesis,* vol. 1. Daily Study Bible (Philadelphia: Westminster and Edinburgh: Saint Andrew, 1981).

Gunkel, Hermann. *Genesis,* 3rd ed. Hand-Kommentar zum Alten Testament I/1 (Göttingen: Vandenhoeck & Ruprecht, 1910).

Kidner, Derek. *Genesis.* Tyndale Old Testament Commentaries (Downers Grove: Inter-Varsity and London: Tyndale, 1967).

Knight, G. A. F. *Theology in Pictures: A Commentary on Genesis, Chapters One to Eleven* (Edinburgh: Handsel, 1981).

Luther, Martin. *Luther's Works.* Vol. 1: *Lectures on Genesis Chapters 1-5* (St. Louis: Concordia, 1958); Vol. 2: *Lectures on Genesis Chapters 6-14 (St. Louis: Concordia, 1960).*

Plaut, W. Gunther. *The Torah: A Modern Commentary.* Vol. 1: *Genesis* (New York: Union of American Hebrew Congregations, 1974).

von Rad, Gerhard. *Genesis,* rev. ed. Old Testament Library (Philadelphia: Westminster and London: SCM, 1972).

Richardson, Alan. *Genesis I-XI,* 3rd ed. Torch Bible Commentaries (London: SCM, 1959).

Skinner, John. *A Critical and Exegetical Commentary on Genesis,* 2nd ed. International Critical Commentary (Edinburgh: T. & T. Clark, 1930).

Speiser, Ephraim A. *Genesis,* 3rd ed. Anchor Bible 1 (Garden City: Doubleday, 1979).

Vawter, Bruce. *On Genesis: A New Reading* (Garden City: Doubleday, 1977).

Westermann, Claus. *Genesis 1–11: A Commentary* (Minneapolis: Augsburg and London: SPCK, 1984).

Other Books

Anderson, Bernhard W., ed. *Creation in the Old Testament*. Issues in Religion and Theology (Philadelphia: Fortress and London: SPCK, 1984).

Barth, Karl. *Church Dogmatics*. Vol. III: *The Doctrine of Creation*, Part One (Edinburgh: T. & T. Clark, 1958).

Bonhoeffer, Dietrich. *Creation and Fall; Temptation* (New York: Macmillan and London: SCM, 1966).

Eliade, Mircea. *Patterns in Comparative Religions* (New York: Sheed & Ward, 1963).

———. *The Sacred and the Profane* (1961; repr. Magnolia, MA: Peter Smith, 1983).

Ellis, Peter F. *The Yahwist: The Bible's First Theologian* (Notre Dame: Fides, 1968).

Frazer, James G. *Folk-Lore in the Old Testament: Studies in Comparative Religion, Legend and Law,* abridged ed. (New York: Macmillan, 1923).

Fretheim, Terence E. *Creation, Fall, and Flood: Studies in Genesis 1-11* (Minneapolis: Augsburg, 1969).

Gilkey, Langdon. *Maker of Heaven and Earth: The Christian Doctrine of Creation in the Light of Modern Knowledge* (1965; repr. Lanham, MD: University Press of America, 1986).

Miller, Patrick D., Jr. *Genesis 1-11: Studies in Structure and Theme*. Journal for the Study of the Old Testament, Supplement 8 (Sheffield: JSOT Press, 1978).

Niditch, Susan. *Chaos to Cosmos: Studies in Biblical Patterns of Creation*. Studies in the Humanities 6 (Chico, CA: Scholars Press, 1985).

Renckens, Henricus. *Israel's Concept of the Beginning: The Theology of Genesis 1-3* (New York: Herder & Herder, 1964).

Ricoeur, Paul. *The Symbolism of Evil* (New York: Harper and Row, 1967).

Sarna, Nahum M. *Understanding Genesis: The Heritage of Biblical Israel* (New York: Jewish Theological Seminary, 1966).

Thielicke, Helmut. *How the World Began: Man in the First Chapters of the Bible* (Philadelphia: Muhlenberg, 1961).

Westermann, Claus. *Creation* (Philadelphia: Fortress and London: SPCK, 1974).